Editor
Lorin Klistoff, M.A.

Managing Editors
Karen Goldfluss, M.S. Ed.
Elizabeth Morris, Ph.D.

Editor-in-Chief
Sharon Coan, M.S. Ed.

Cover Artist
Barb Lorseyedi

Illustrator
Kevin McCarthy

Art Manager
Kevin Barnes

Art Director
CJae Froshay

Imaging
Rosa C. See

Product Manager
Phil Garcia

Publishers
Rachelle Cracchiolo, M.S. Ed.
Mary Dupuy Smith, M.S. Ed.

GRAPHIC ORGANIZERS

Grades K–3

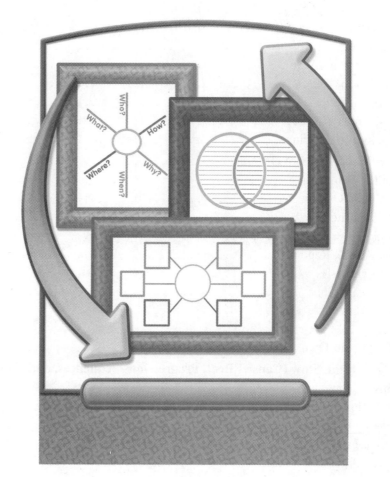

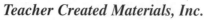

Author

Casey Null Petersen

Teacher Created Materials, Inc.
6421 Industry Way
Westminster, CA 92683
www.teachercreated.com

ISBN-0-7439-3207-2

©2004 Teacher Created Materials, Inc.

Made in U.S.A.

Table of Contents

Table of Contents

Introduction

We all use graphic organizers of some kind, and to some degree, every day of our lives. A menu, a train schedule, a calendar, and even a guide to television programs are all examples of graphic organizers. They are beneficial in making it possible for us to visualize information in a condensed and organized form. They also make it possible for us to organize plans, thoughts, and ideas. They help writers to organize thoughts before writing. They are the tools that help us to learn, process information, envision, and create.

If students become familiar with graphic organizers at an early age, they are more likely to have an understanding of how to organize ideas and concepts, how to think more clearly, how to plan with a goal in mind, and how to relate concepts, ideas, and facts to other concepts, ideas and facts. Learners, of all kinds, are better able to visualize information and ideas when familiar with graphic organizers. They are better able to access information, understand information, and organize and present information.

There are a variety of graphic organizers included in this book, and a variety of ways to use them. The organizers are arranged according to their types and similarities, but many graphic organizers may be used for multi-purposes. Any graphic organizer may be modified (expanded, simplified, or combined) to suit student capabilities, the intended purposes of the organizer, or an entirely new use. The organizers may be reproduced, copied after being modified, used individually, in groups, or enlarged for whole class use.

Each section begins with an introduction offering suggestions for the uses of its graphic organizers. In addition, the simpler organizers are nearer the beginning of each section progressing to the more complex toward the end. Nevertheless, the graphic organizers in this book can be modified so that they are suitable to younger and older students. Some suggestions for ways to do this are found in the introductions.

Some organizers come with filled-in examples, but that does not mean that the organizer can only be used in that manner and with that kind of subject matter. Some organizers come with very little direction, in part because they may be such common organizers that their usage is well known and they are included so that they may be readily accessible, and in part because some organizers are open-ended enough that your own interpretation, and the interpretations of the students, is encouraged.

Creativity is also encouraged. With familiarity with the organizers in this book, it is hoped that students and teachers will feel competent in creating new, useful, and specific organizers for their own needs. Learning is often fluid and organic, and so, organizers to facilitate such processes ought to also be organic and fluid. Graphic organizers can be created on the fly, as it were, while in process and in need of a way to structure what is being created, imagined, or analyzed.

Some kinds of organizers appear more than once in the book, with different purposes in mind. Even then, the uses of graphic organizers are not limited to only those purposes, and perhaps could be placed in every section of the book with some modification.

This book offers only a few of the many graphic organizers available. In addition, there are those that you are inspired to create after having experience with these. Each graphic organizer can be modified, combined, or revised to fit the needs of students and the lessons being prepared. While there is some overlap between the books, for graphic organizers more suitable for older students, see TCM #3208, *Graphic Organizers Grades 4–8.*

Web Spinning

This section begins with *Brainstorming Rules* (page 6). Two lists are included. One is a simplified version for students to refer to as a reminder. They may each have a copy at their desks, or put the rules on a poster near the chalkboard or whiteboard. The value in brainstorming is to allow the ideas to flow without judgment. One idea will lead to another and one student's train of thought will inspire another's. Brainstorm for topics, ideas, and inspiration.

An organizer for using the results of a brainstorming session follows, *Brainstorming Organizer I* (page 7). It is not, however, the only way or the best way to record brainstorming results. Perhaps a brainstorming session to create a brainstorming results organizer is in order! *Brainstorming Organizer II* (page 8) could be used after a session, when the best ideas are chosen, or during the session, as a means of recording the ideas as they come. It is important to record every idea that is presented during brainstorming.

The webs that follow, in this section, can be used in many ways to introduce students to the concept of creating webs. *Organizing the Results* (page 9), is a chart that includes four columns for sorting the results of a brainstorming session. The chart can be adapted for fewer or more columns, as needed. Again, this graphic organizer is best used during or immediately following a brainstorming session. One idea would be to have the teacher, or a student, writing the ideas as they come, on the board, while another records them on a graphic organizer. An alternative would be to have all students recording on a graphic organizer during the session. But only the latter is not recommended for beginning brainstormers. They need to be able to focus on what is happening during the session. A simple, generic web for brainstorming is included on page 10, *Brainstorming Web*.

Word Web (page 11) is a simple and useful way to introduce young students to webs, in general, as they improve their vocabularies. Students may also use the web for defining science or social studies words. The *Senses Web*, on page 12, offers additional web practice for students, and can be used in a variety of ways, such as creative writing, reporting on field trips, science, etc. Try introducing students to the Senses Web by having them record what they sense in the immediate moment, in the classroom.

The *5 Ws and 1 H Web* (page 13) is useful in many areas of the curriculum, reinforcing both the Ws and Hs and organizational thinking skills. Familiarity with the graphic organizer will cause the students to think of the Ws and Hs any time they write, or inquire, or research.

The Web Spinning section ends with *Freeform Clustering* (page 16), a method for recording and generating ideas. Clustering is most effective in creative writing, but it can also generate ideas for reports, projects, and any subjects that need fresh ideas. (See example on pages 14 and 15). A student who has had practice with freeform clustering will be more capable of generating ideas and structure when asked to write.

Brainstorming Rules

How to Brainstorm

1. Write down every thought and idea. Every thought and idea has value.
2. Record thoughts and ideas very quickly. Keep things moving with a rapid flow of ideas.
3. Do not interrupt the flow to judge any thoughts or ideas. Record all thoughts even if they seem off topic, unrelated, or even dumb.
4. Remember that ideas that do not seem worth recording might prove to be important after all. At the very least, they may lead to other valuable ideas.
5. Brainstorming can be done alone, but the more people involved in the process, the more ideas will be generated.
6. Keep brainstorming until the ideas slow down. Take a deep breath, pause, and be ready to record some more ideas. They will still trickle in for a while.
7. When the ideas finally seem to slow to a stop, look over what was generated.
8. Choose the best ideas to use.

The Rules of Brainstorming

- ✎ Write down everything.
- ✎ Write fast.
- ✎ Don't stop for any reason.
- ✎ All ideas are valuable.
- ✎ Brainstorm alone, but even better, with others.
- ✎ Keep brainstorming. Pause but don't quit yet.
- ✎ When finished, look at what is written.
- ✎ Choose the best ideas.

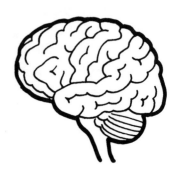

    6

Brainstorming Organizer I

T O P I C

I D E A S

Web Spinning (Brainstorms, Clusters, and Webs)

Brainstorming Organizer II

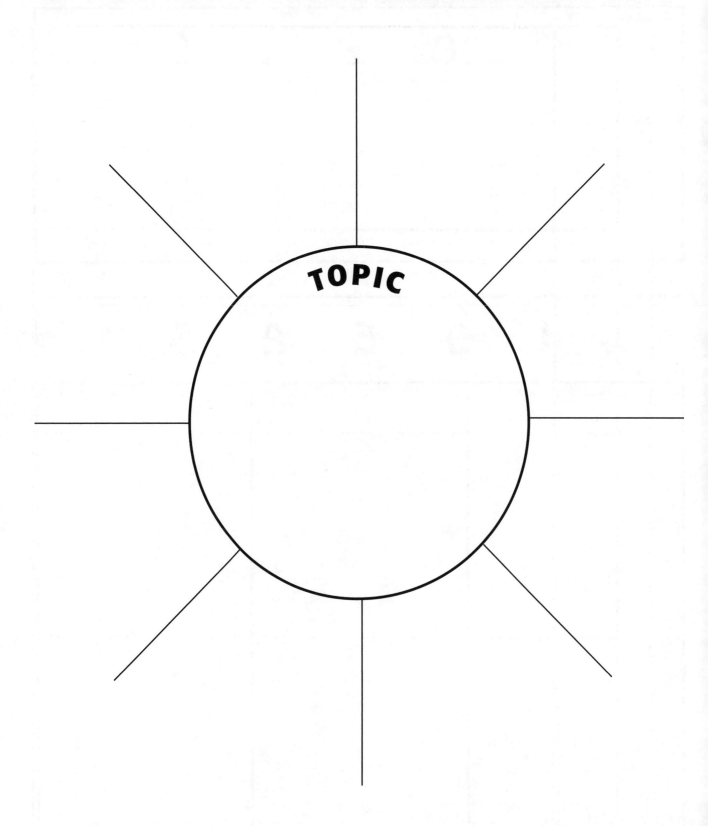

TOPIC

 **Organizing the Results**

Brainstorming Web

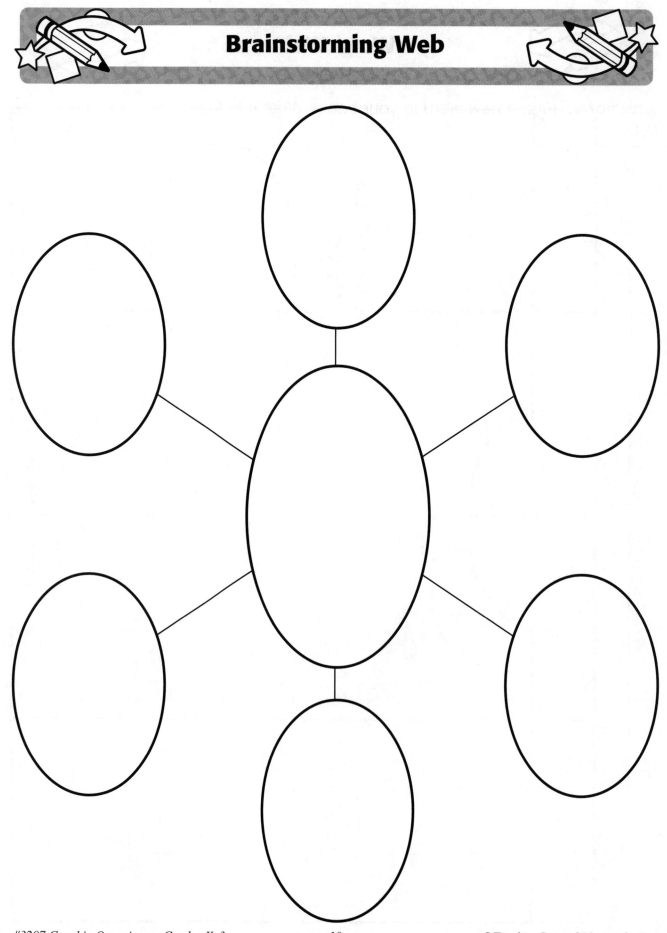

Word Web

Directions: Find a new word in your book. Write it in the center oval. Fill in the web.

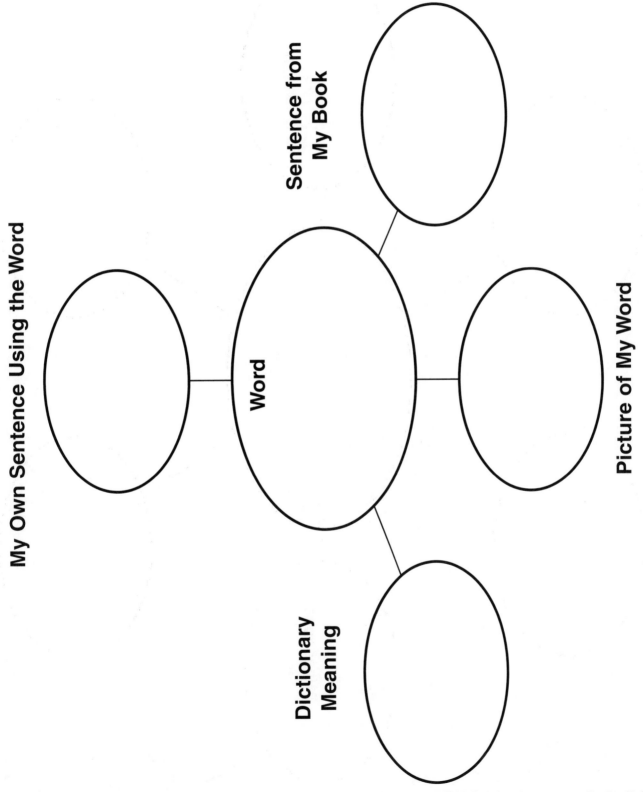

Sentence from My Book

My Own Sentence Using the Word

Word

Picture of My Word

Dictionary Meaning

Senses Web

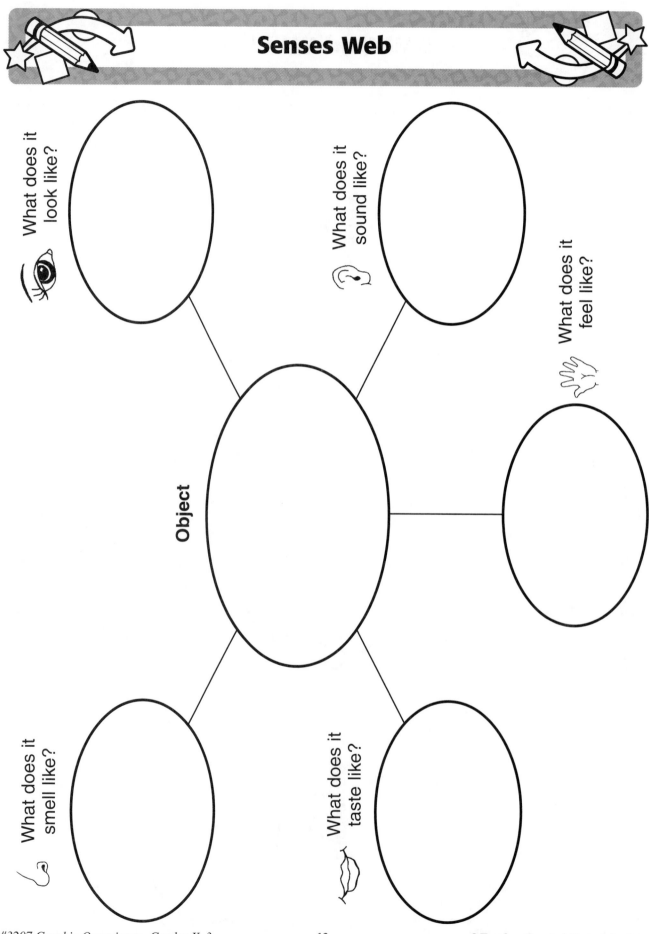

What does it look like?

What does it sound like?

What does it feel like?

Object

What does it smell like?

What does it taste like?

5 Ws and 1 H Web

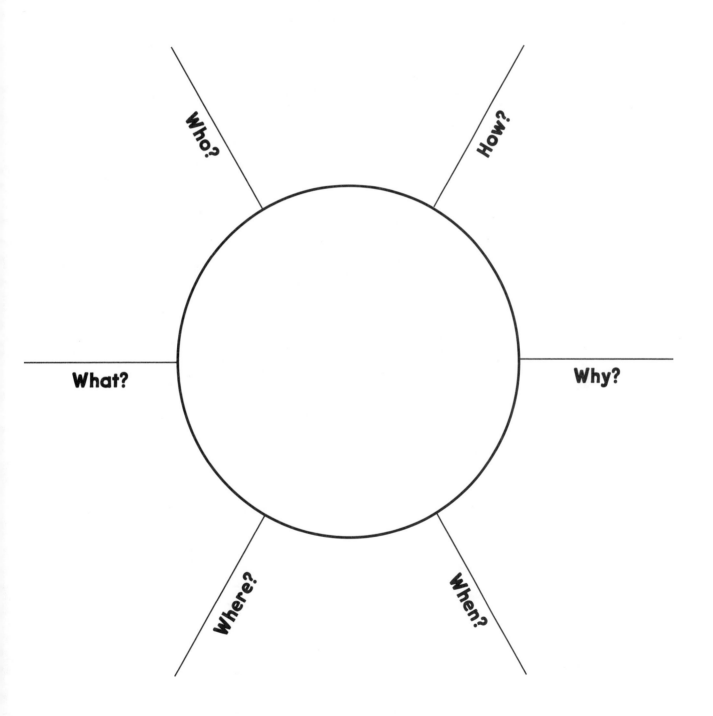

Who?

How?

What?

Why?

Where?

When?

Freeform Clustering

Freeform clusters grow along with your ideas. Begin with a topic, such as "Summer." Create clusters that grow from your topic such as the ones below.

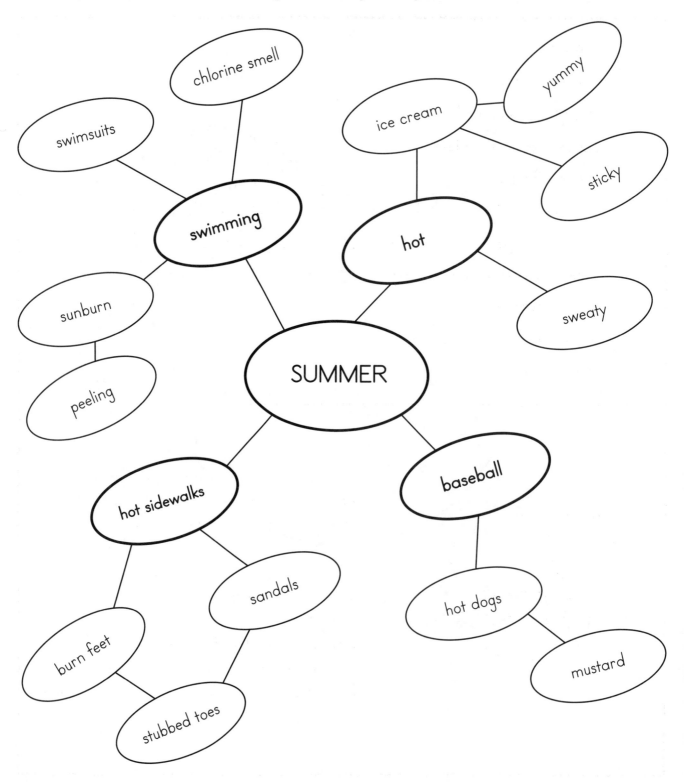

Freeform Clustering

When finished clustering, you can write a poem or a story from the cluster. Here are some examples of writing from the cluster on page 14.

Summer

Summer sizzles

Skin's hot; sunburned

Sidewalk blisters my feet

Sandals flip flop

Ice cream soothes

Baseball's super

Tangy mustard on my hot dog

Slip into swimsuit

Swimming's cool

Summer soothes.

Summer

I love summer. I wake up and get on my bike until I am all sweaty from riding on the hot sidewalks to get ice cream. It is yummy and sticky as it melts and drips down my arms. Then I go to play baseball and then for a swim. Ahh, I walk in sandals in the grass, eating a hotdog on the Fourth of July, watching the sizzling fireworks and then feeling all cozy and sunburned as I go to sleep dreaming of what I will do for fun the next day.

Freeform Clustering

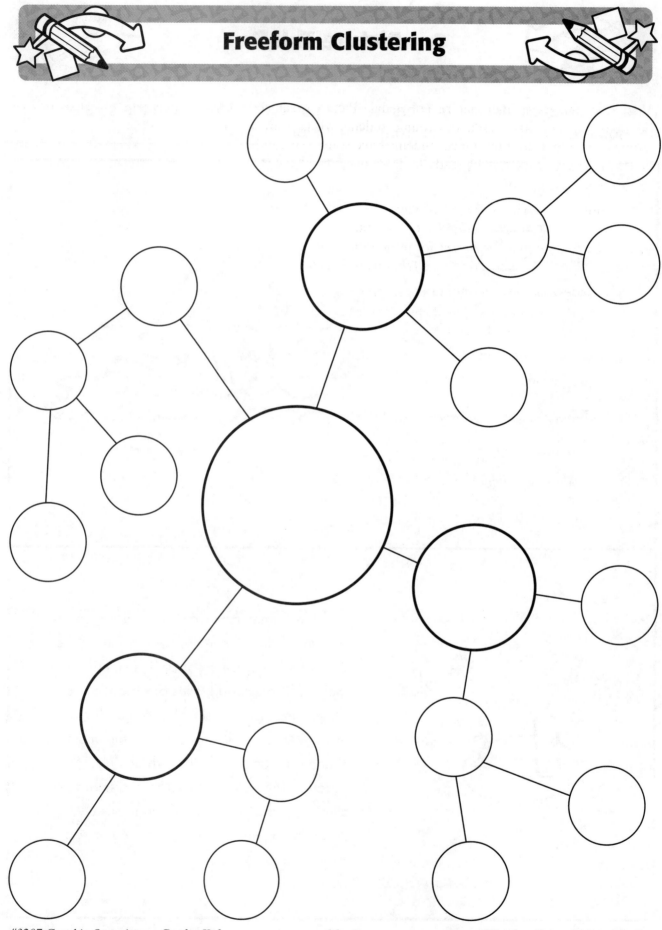

Picture This!

Graphic organizers, by their nature, are visual. Picture organizers make this even more of an asset. Picture organizers are beneficial to young students, visual learners, and students of all ages and abilities. And they are fun! Once students have some experience with them, encourage them to create their own. They will likely be ready to do so once they have worked with some of the picture organizers in this section.

This section begins with *Spider Web* (page 18)—a simple web in the shape of, of course, a spider. Instruct students to write a main idea on the spider's body and to use its legs for the details. This would be a good graphic organizer for prewriting a spooky story in October. Students will long remember how this organizer arranged the main topic and its supporting points.

The *Umbrella Organizer* that follows (page 19) is another variation of the main idea and what branches off from it. To reinforce teaching, hang a real or cardboard umbrella from the ceiling. Label the umbrella with a main point, and let the details dangle from its spokes.

My Favorite Words, on page 20, will offer students a graphic experience as they connect words with art and organize it all in a cohesive manner. Encourage them to create new shapes for other kinds of words. They might want to each create a personal, Favorite Words book complete with shapes and colors to present the words. Tie in the word choices with subjects being studied.

Book Cover (page 21) may also be used for book reports, or to inspire students to create their own stories. Another book report option would be *Fishy Book Report* (page 22). This graphic organizer can be recreated with other themes and for other subjects as well. Have students draw shapes that tie in with the genre of the books they read.

Students have another opportunity to reinforce the *5 Ws and 1 H* concept, but this time in a visually memorable way, as they fill in the shapes on page 23, that should make things very clear to visual learners. *Ice Cream Cone* (page 24) is a graphic organizer that will help young learners to visualize how writing and thinking is organized. Keeping the pleasant image in mind, they will grow in their competencies. Before introducing the organizer, bring in some plain cones and ask them what is missing. Ask the students if they would like the plain cones, or if they would prefer them to have the "details" added.

Similarly, the *Word Bank* on page 25, will help students to understand how their vocabularies grow in a manner not unlike their piggy banks. Enlarge the piggy bank drawing and place it on a wall in the classroom and have students add new words for a whole class piggy bank.

While the *Family Tree* (page 26) is well suited to organizing family information, it may also be used for organizing other kinds of information. Have blank trees on hand for other subjects, as well. Read aloud an enjoyable story, and have the class organize its information on a tree graph with the main idea and or main characters on the tree trunk and the supporting details on the branches.

With *Create Your Own* (pages 27 and 28), encourage students to create their own picture organizers. Have brainstorming sessions, for instance, to come up with uses for picture organizers, and then, perhaps a session for what kinds of picture organizers could be created to display the information. Have a gallery showing for picture organizers with each student submitting an original idea. After the showing, make enough copies of each so that each student will have a notebook full of original class picture organizers.

Spider Web

Umbrella Organizer

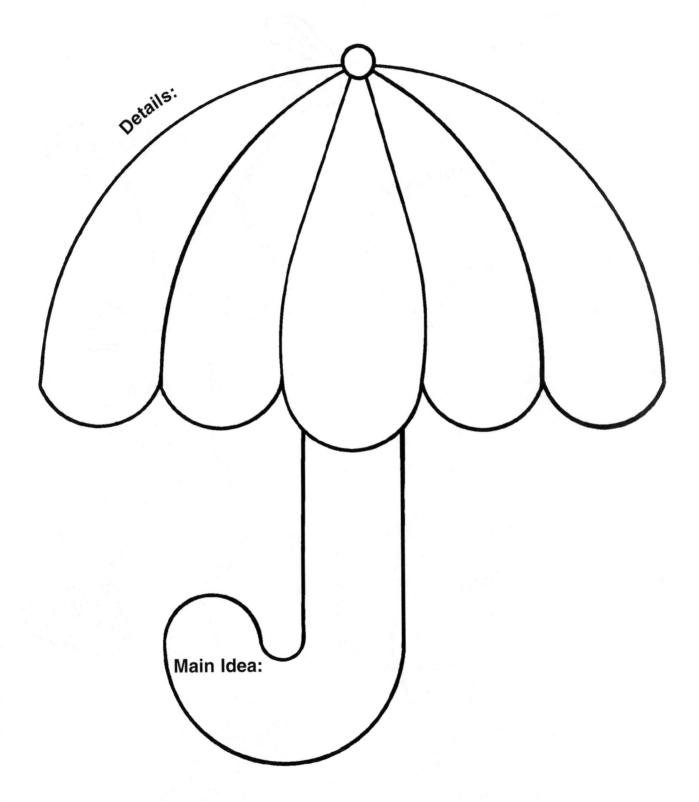

Details:

Main Idea:

My Favorite Words

Yummy Words

Sleepy Words

Happy Words

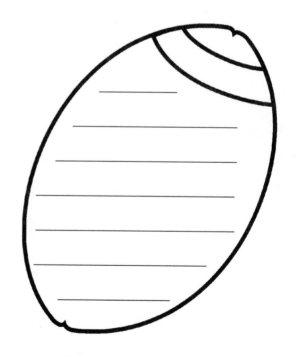

Active Words

20

Book Cover

Fishy Book Report

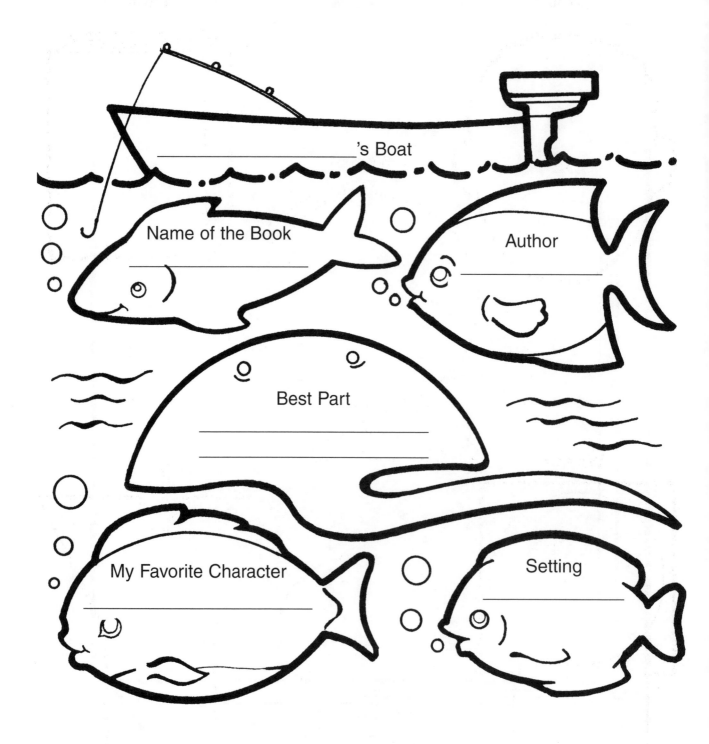

_____'s Boat

Name of the Book

_____

Author

_____

Best Part

_____

My Favorite Character

_____

Setting

_____

5 Ws and 1 H

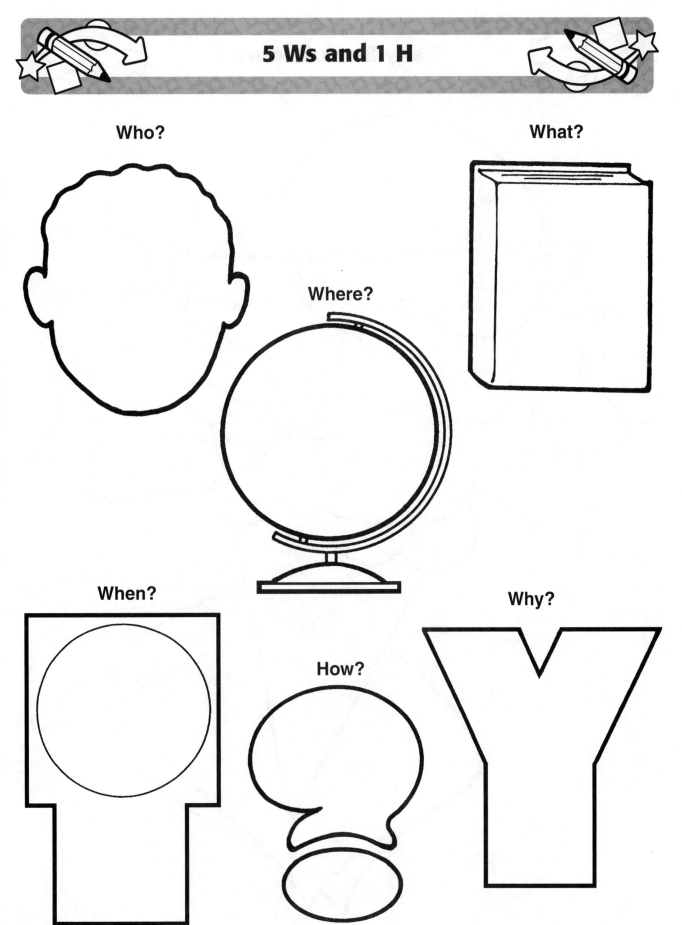

Who?

What?

Where?

When?

How?

Why?

Ice Cream Cone

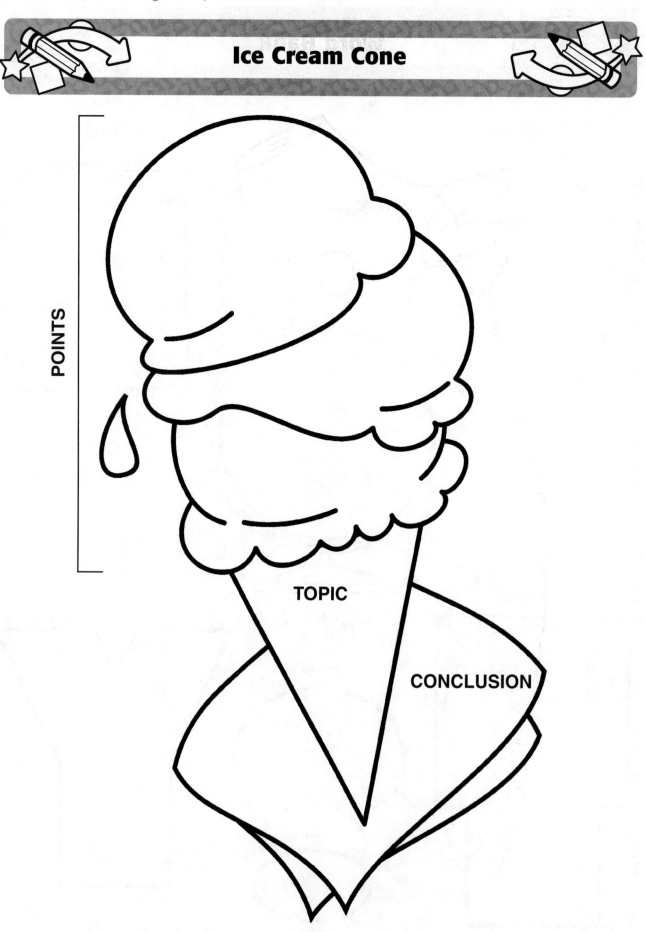

POINTS

TOPIC

CONCLUSION

Word Bank

Directions: Collect all the words you can on a subject and "deposit" them in the "bank" below.

Topic: _____

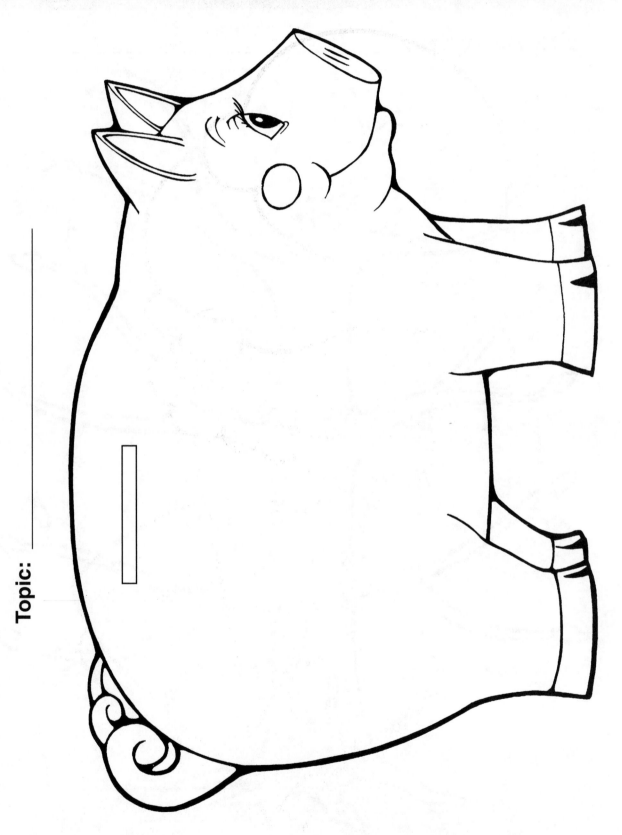

Family Tree

My Family Name: _____

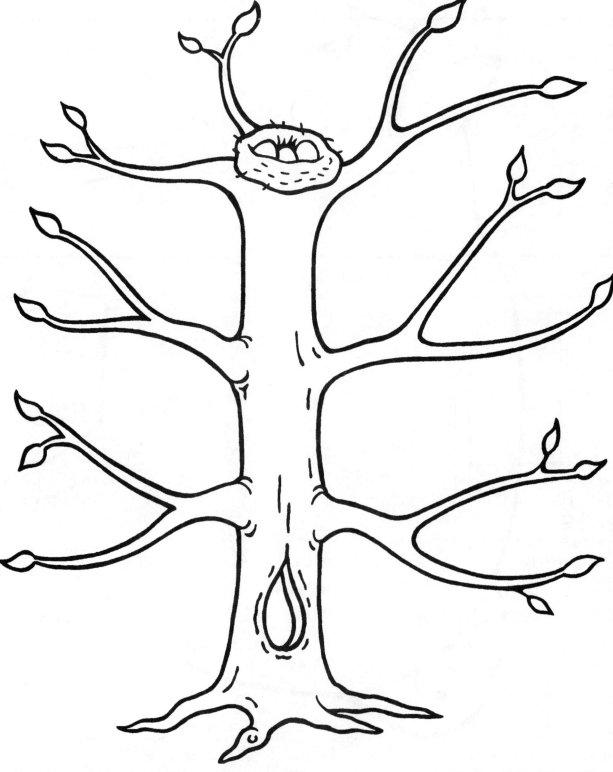

Create Your Own

There are many ways to create your own picture organizers. You can draw a picture of yourself standing in a park, or by the shore of a lake or river, or on a mountain, and then add all that you see, smell, hear, etc. Here is an example:

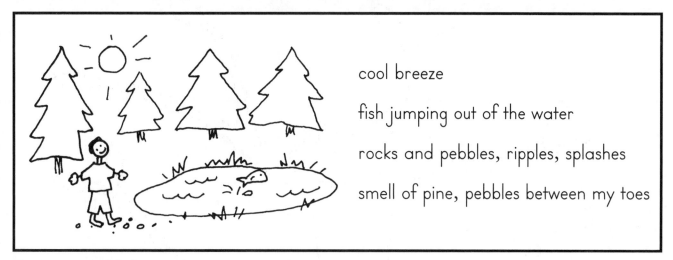

cool breeze

fish jumping out of the water

rocks and pebbles, ripples, splashes

smell of pine, pebbles between my toes

Or, you could draw your room to show where you keep everything, like this:

games

clothes

shoes, basketballs

window

socks

bed

books

rock collection

comic books

school books

homework

You might want to create a graphic organizer to help you remember what you need to do each day and each night.

MORNING	AFTERNOON	NIGHT
dog food, water, shower, breakfast	walk dog, practice piano	dog food, homework, brush teeth

Create Your Own

You could create an organizer to help you to remember new words.

New Word	What is it?
aphid	The bug is eating mom's roses.
barbell	The things my dad has under the bed.

Use the space below, or another piece of paper to create your own picture organizer.

 # Going with the Flow

An understanding of the concepts of sequencing, order, and flow will enable students to think more clearly and to organize their thoughts in a fashion that will make them more readily expressed to others. This section begins with a simple graphic organizer that will be very useful to them. The organizer, *This is How I . . .* (page 30) is a simple form for young students to use in sequencing. Have them brainstorm how-to topics (how to bake a cake, how to feed a baby, how to wash the clothes, etc.), choose their topics, and list the steps in order. The process will not only teach them how to organize sequential thoughts, but also the transitional words that are clues in reading and writing. Have the students each choose a topic they wish to present to others ("How I Make a Sandwich," "How I Skate," "How I Wash the Dog," etc.) Using the graphic organizer to think about and list the steps, have them prepare and give their presentations to the class, complete with visual aids. This organizer is followed by another (*First Things First,* page 31) which can be used in a similar manner, with steps written, or drawn. This will be the preferred organizer for some students.

Sequencing becomes even more complex with *Making Progress* (page 32). Show students how there is a flow from one box to the next. Again, this organizer can be used with drawings, as well as written steps. The *Linear Flow Chart* (pages 33 and 34) is useful in giving students practice in many subjects from reporting on their days to putting events in order, such as the stages of growth in a seed. After the linear organizer, there is a *Cycle Organizer* (page 35), which can be used to organize such ideas as the cycle of weather and water, seasons, or whatever students may think of. It will be very useful in demonstrating cycles that might be difficult to explain without such a graphic organizer.

The *Multi-Use Flow Chart* (page 36) may be used for drawing, writing, or both, and more circles may be added or some deleted. Have students think of and list ways that such a flow chart might be useful. Have a brainstorming session to come up with as many uses as possible, not only for students but for many different people with many different kinds of jobs to do.

Several Cause and Effect Organizers follow (pages 37 through 39), beginning with the simple to the more complex. When students are able to graphically visualize cause and effect, as these organizers will facilitate, they will be better prepared to understand concepts in social studies, history, sciences, and literature. In the beginning, suggest some simple cause and effect situations that they may have experienced in their lives (such as what happens when they fight with siblings, are late getting ready for school, do not eat their vegetables, etc.) Use the *Sequencing* organizer (page 40) to help students visualize events that happen one after the other. The *Fishbone* organizer on page 41 will enable students to see how multiple causes can lead to an effect. Sometimes it is difficult for younger students to comprehend such a thing as cause and effect. An organizer that lets them see what would otherwise be invisible to them, is very helpful.

A *Time Line* (page 42) is included in this section, and it can be used in many ways to graph historical as well as personal events. Begin with the simple and the personal: a student's daily schedule, his or her recollection of a family event, what happened on a field trip, etc.

The *Relationship Chart* (page 43) may be used to graph the many interwoven relationships of a character in a book, or it may be used for the relationships a student may have with others. Have students put themselves in the center of the graph and then put friends or relatives in the outer sections. This chart can also organize the relationships between various concepts and ideas when students are ready for more critical thinking.

Going with the Flow (Cause/Effect, Progressions/Sequences, and Flow Charts)

This Is How I . . .

First, _____

_____

_____

Second, _____

_____

_____

Third, _____

_____

_____

Fourth, _____

_____

_____

Last, _____

_____

_____

First Things First

Topic: _____

Making Progress

TOPIC: _____

_____

1

2

4

3

5

6

Linear Flow Chart

Starting Event

 Get up in the morning

Event 1

 Eat breakfast with brother

Event 2

 Eat lunch with friends at school

Event 3

 Eat dinner with family

Final Event

 Go to bed

Linear Flow Chart

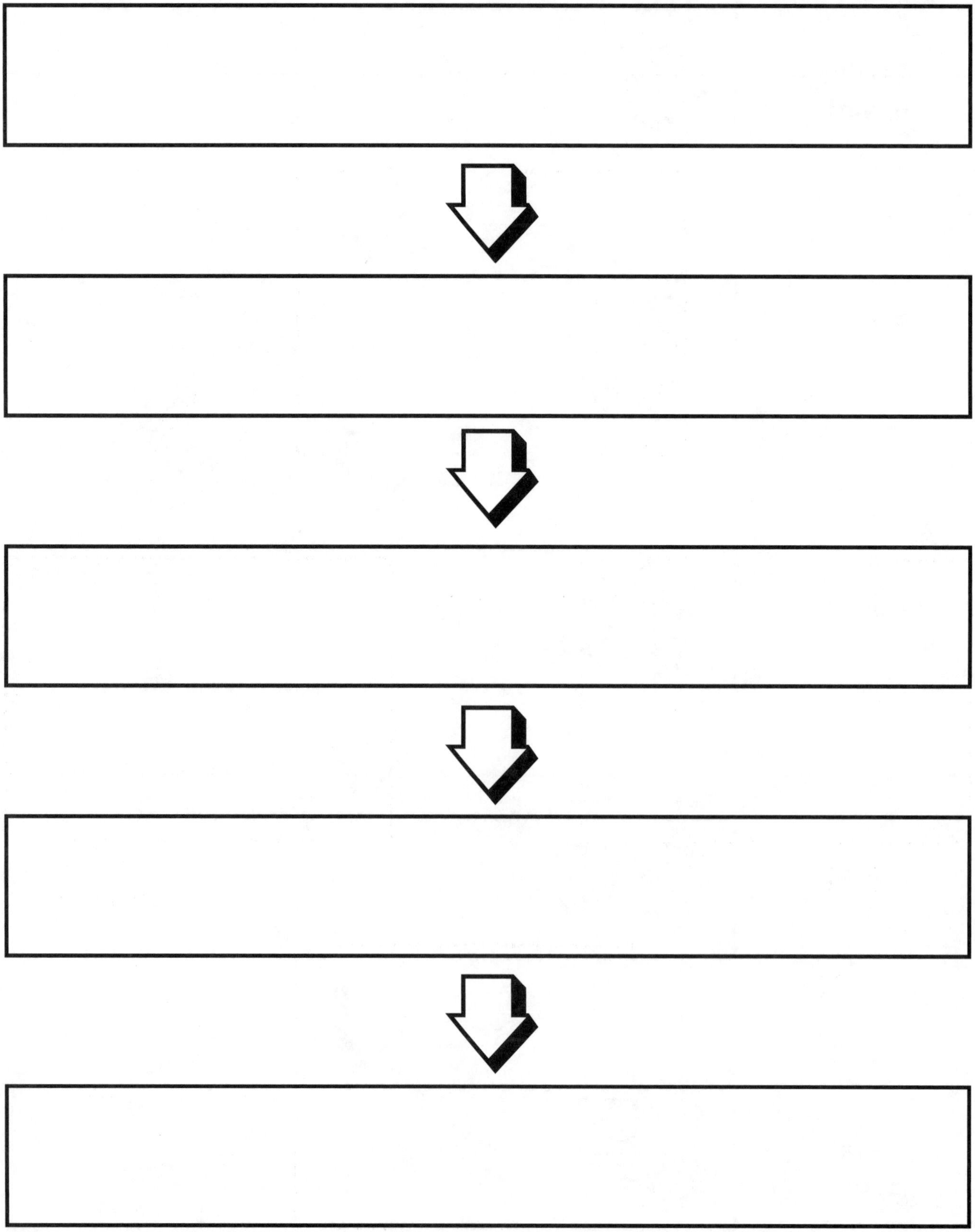

[ ]

⬇

[ ]

⬇

[ ]

⬇

[ ]

⬇

[ ]

Cycle Organizer

_____

(type of cycle)

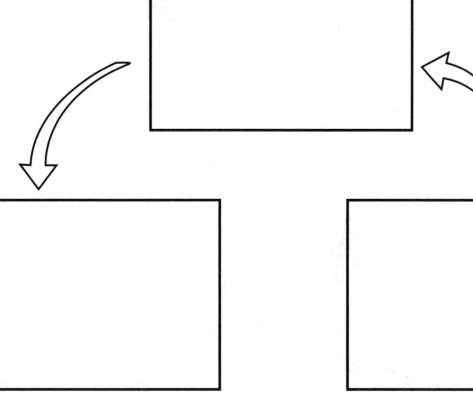

Multi-Use Flow Chart

TOPIC: _____

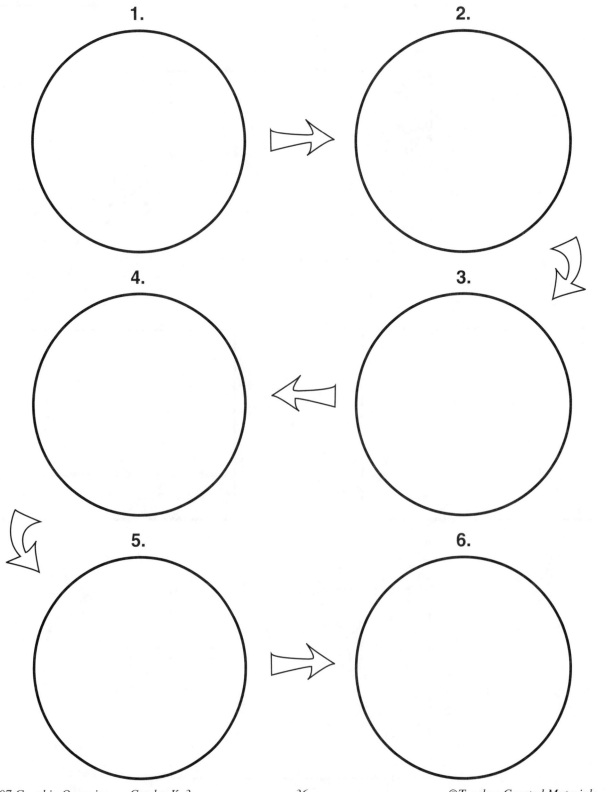

Cause and Effect I

Topic: _____

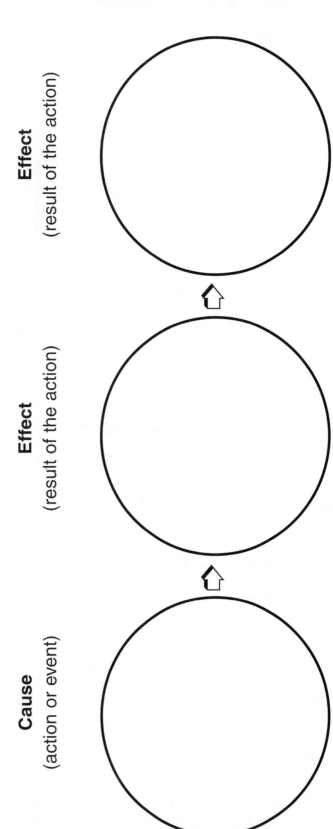

Effect
(result of the action)

Effect
(result of the action)

Cause
(action or event)

Cause and Effect II

CAUSE

EFFECT

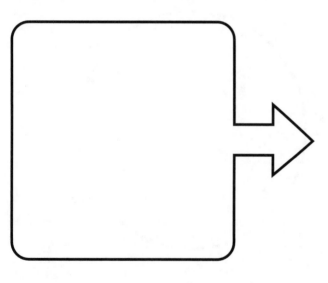

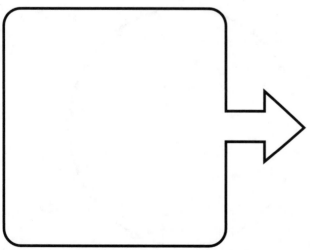

Cause and Effect III

This event

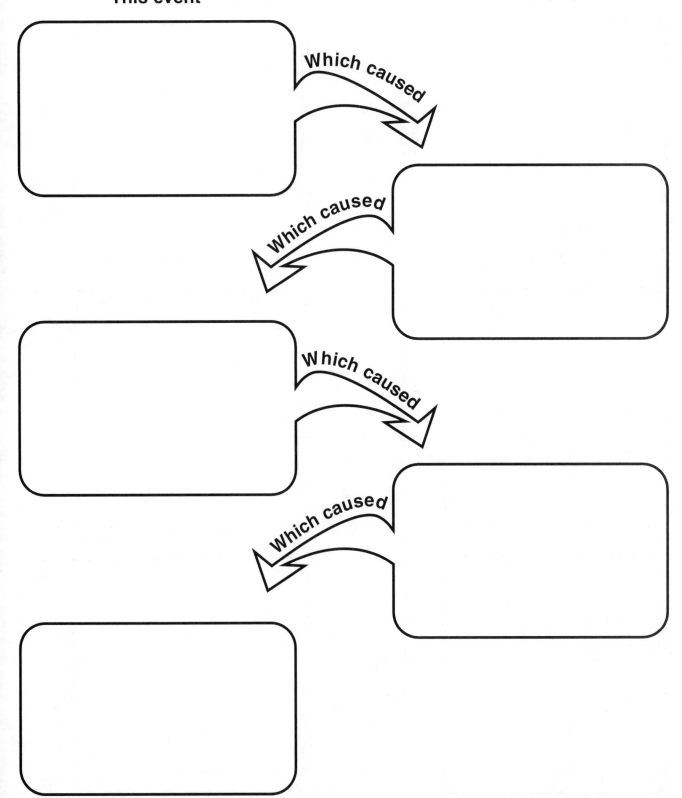

Sequencing

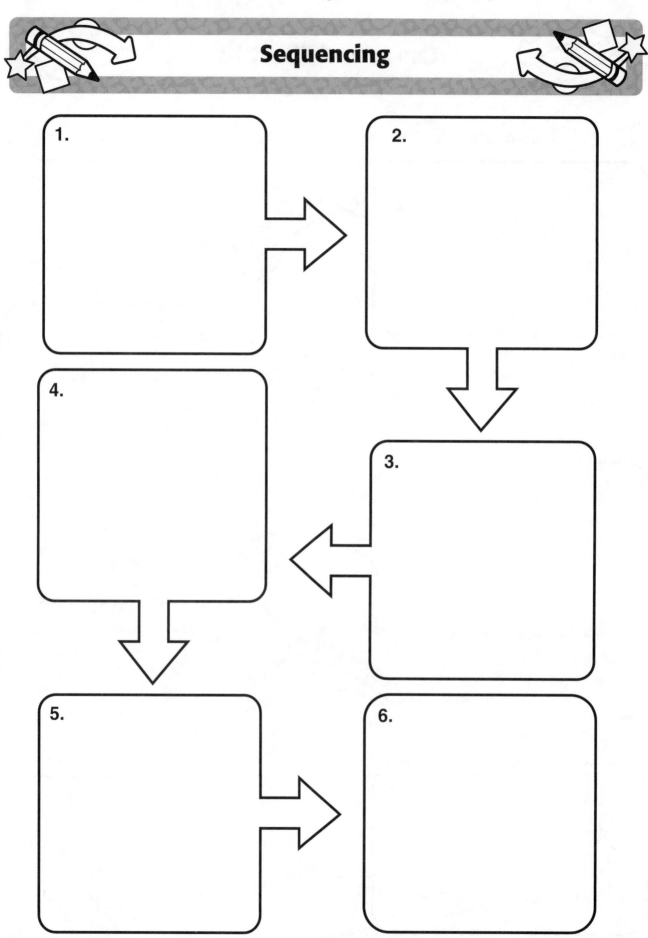

1.

2.

4.

3.

5.

6.

Fishbone

Directions: Choose the most important effect, or event that happens. Write this effect on the line labeled "Effect." Then find the four most important things that caused this effect. Write each of these on a line that says "Cause."

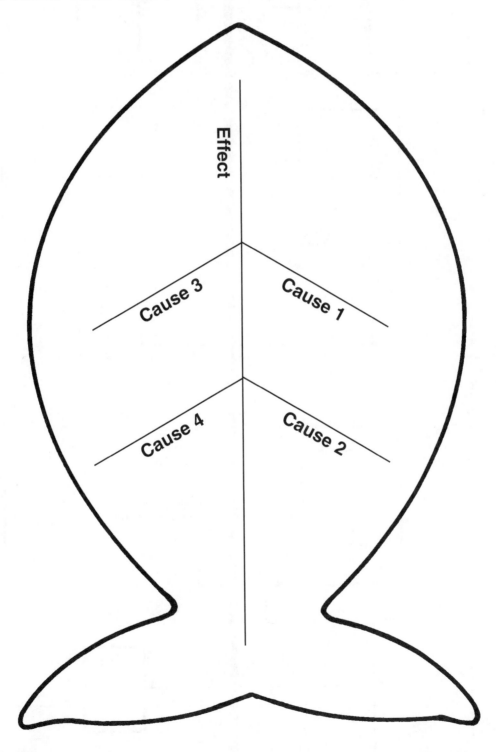

Time Line

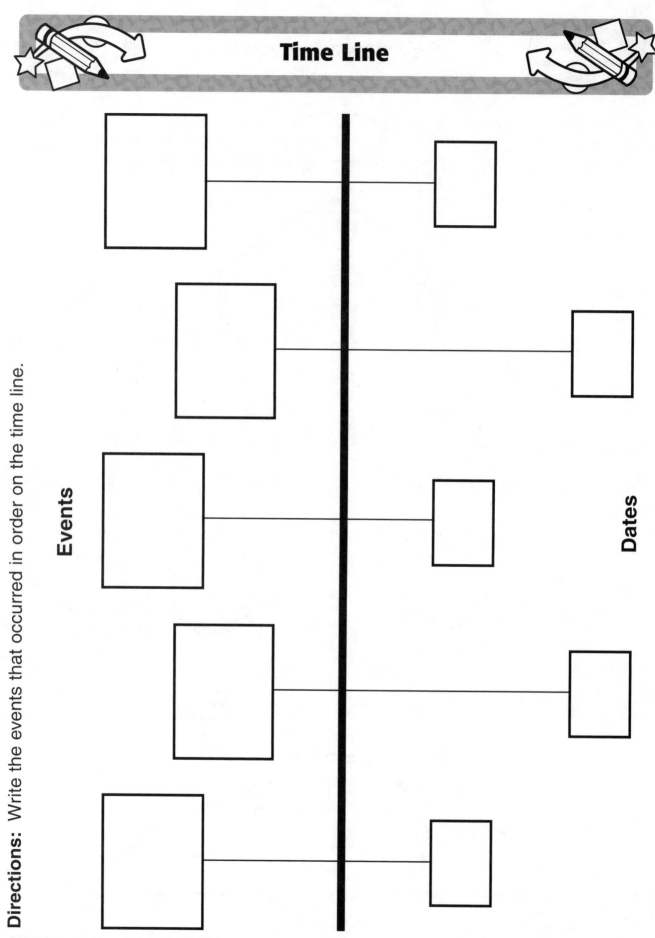

Directions: Write the events that occurred in order on the time line.

Events

Dates

Relationship Chart

On the Other Hand . . .

The ability to compare and contrast is an essential critical thinking skill, and as the years progress it will become more and more important. Students will need to be able to compare and contrast, and they will need to be able to write clear and strong comparison and contrast essays. In addition, students with skills in this area are better able to make decisions and solve problems.

This section begins with a simple *Comparison Matrix* (page 45), which will enable students to become capable at comparisons, by using familiar topics. Create similar organizers to allow students to gain competency in comparing and contrasting. Students may be willing to create their own comparison matrices, once they become familiar with them, their ease of use, and how effective they can be. The matrix is followed by several comparison and contrast organizers: *Compare and Contrast Chart* (page 46), *Compare and Contrast Grid* (page 47), and *Compare and Contrast List* (page 48) which can be used in a variety of ways according to student ability and interest. These organizers will enable students to gain critical thinking skills as well.

Different and Alike (page 49) is useful as an introduction of the Venn diagram concept. No matter our age or experience, it is always more efficient to compare two things when they can be graphically presented. Page 50, *How to Read a Venn Diagram*, introduces students to the much-used Venn diagram with an activity to familiarize them. A *Numbers Venn Diagram* is found on page 51, and *Making a Venn Diagram* about the weather is found on page 52. They are examples of ways it can be used with different subjects. A blank *Venn Diagram* (page 53) is included to be used across the curriculum. Once students are capable of making comparisons and finding contrasts, they will be ready to deal with problem solving and decisions.

A *Problem and Solution Organizer* is found on page 54. Students will find it useful in many ways. In class, discuss many kinds of problems (there are those of fictional characters, those of the students, those of the school, and those of the world). Discuss the ways in which the organizer, or one like it, can help someone define the problem and think of solutions. *How Do I Decide?* (page 55), will help students to not only define just what it is that they need to solve, but how to find a solution. Emphasize the portion about how to find a solution. Students gain competency when they understand that there are ways to seek answers and solutions.

Since this section begins with a Comparison Matrix, it is only fitting that it concludes with a *Thinking Matrix* (page 56). Once students have had some experience with comparing and contrasting in a variety of ways, they will be capable of organizing their thoughts in order to be able to make choices. Have students create their own Comparison and Thinking Matrices. They can also create symbols to make picture matrices.

Comparison Matrix

SAMPLE

	Go to School	Read	Walk	Laugh
Me	✓	✓	✓	✓
Baby Sister				✓
Dad		✓	✓	✓
Grandma		✓		✓

Compare and Contrast Chart

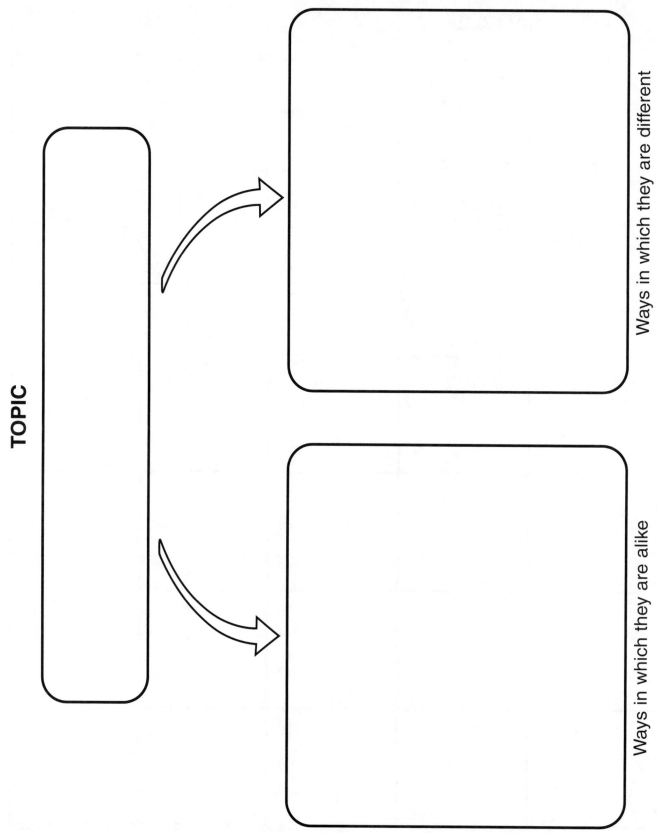

TOPIC

Ways in which they are different

Ways in which they are alike

Compare and Contrast Grid

Topic: _____

Items Being Compared →

Topics for Comparison →

Compare and Contrast List

Topic: _____

Alike	Different
_____	_____
_____	_____
_____	_____
_____	_____
_____	_____
_____	_____

Summary: _____

_____

Different and Alike

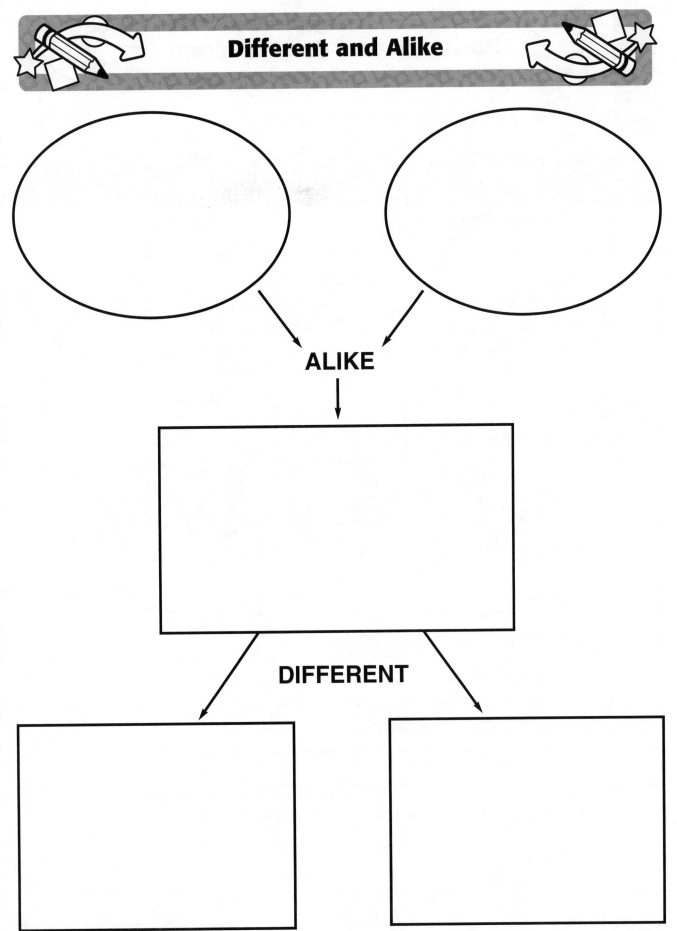

ALIKE

DIFFERENT

How to Read a Venn Diagram

Use the Venn diagram below to answer the questions.

Cartoon People and Real People

Cartoon People

- Never get older
- If flattened by a steamroller, get right back up
- Often have dog noses and tails
- Have super powers

Both

- Talk
- Have eyes and hands
- Have problems to solve
- Get into trouble

Real People

- Can really get hurt
- Are real
- Need rest, water, and food
- Have real feelings

1. List three things about cartoon people. _____

_____

_____

2. List three things about real people. _____

_____

_____

3. List three things that are the same about cartoon and real people.

_____

_____

_____

Numbers Venn Diagram

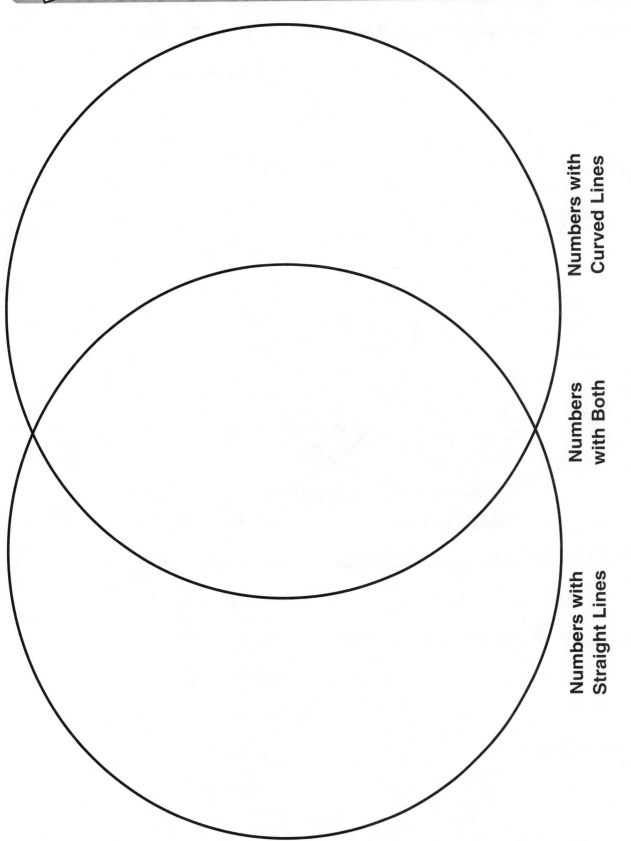

**Numbers with
Curved Lines**

**Numbers
with Both**

**Numbers with
Straight Lines**

Making a Venn Diagram

Comparing a Rainy Day to a Sunny Day

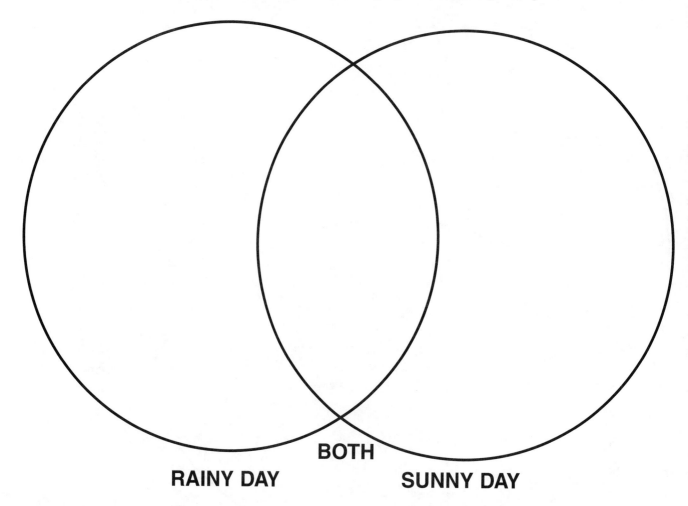

BOTH

RAINY DAY   **SUNNY DAY**

Put the information below into the correct areas of the Venn diagram.

- Play in puddles
- Stay inside and drink hot chocolate
- Play games
- Get wet
- Do homework

- Play outside
- Plant a garden
- Go swimming
- Read a book
- Talk on the telephone

Venn Diagram

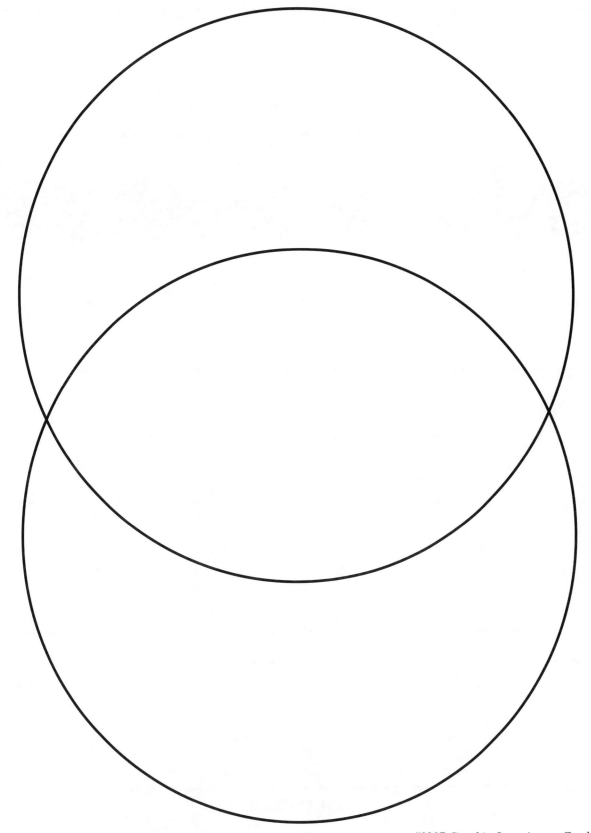

Problem and Solution Organizer

PROBLEM

+ PROS +	– CONS –

SOLUTION

How Do I Decide?

HOW DO I DECIDE?

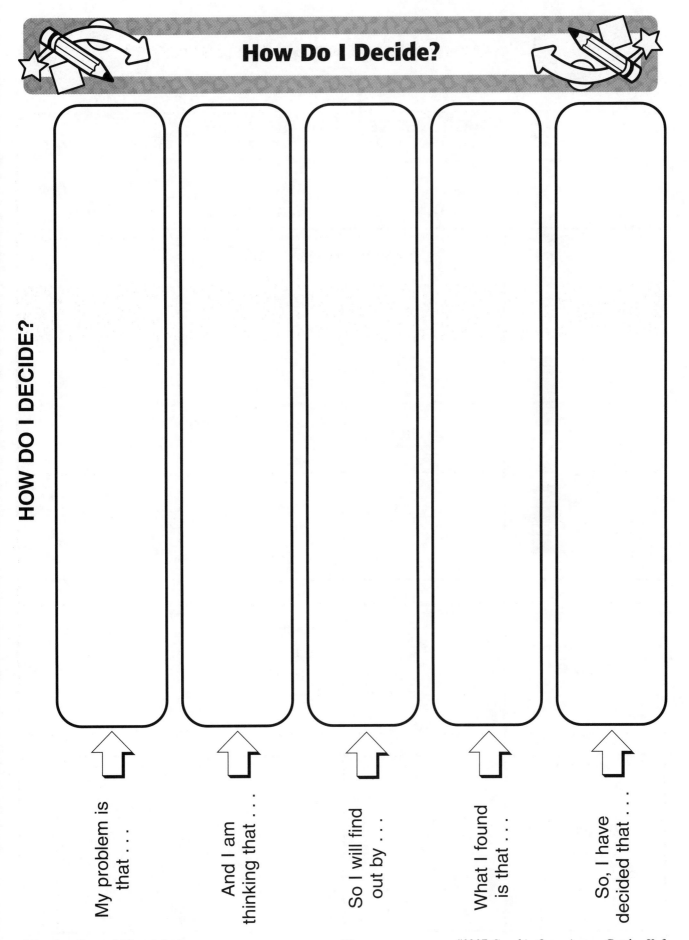

My problem is that . . .

And I am thinking that . . .

So I will find out by . . .

What I found is that . . .

So, I have decided that . . .

Thinking Matrix

Which Dessert Should I Have?

	Taste	Availability	Best for me to eat
Pie	☆ yummy	There is a pie on the kitchen counter. ☆ ☆ ☆	
Ice cream	☆ yummy	Would have to go and buy it ☹	
Cookies	☆ ☆ ☆ very yummy	Would have to make them ☹	
Bowl of fruit			Most nutritious ☆ ☆ ☆

Would You Like Another Piece?

Students will be able to sink their teeth into this section as various forms of graphs make it easy for them to visualize and organize information. Pie graphs enable students to readily access quantitative information. Students come pre-equipped with an interest in who gets the largest piece of the pie. A pizza pie, made from colorful construction paper and appropriately labeled, can help students to comprehend fractions, percentages, and other math concepts including amounts of time, portions of a whole, or preferences. If possible, a demonstration with a real piece of pie, or a bar graph cut into a flat pan of baked goodies will make the learning even more memorable. This section begins with a pie graph dividing up a student's daytime hours (*How I Spend My Day*, page 58). Have students think about and list prior to filling in their graphs. A class discussion may also be in order as many students may assume that school takes one-half to three-quarters of the pie.

This graph is followed, on page 59, with a simple bar graph, *Our Favorite Colors*. As a class activity, have students prepare the information beforehand. There are many topics to use on a bar graph. Favorites are a logical choice for younger students: favorite colors, foods, pets, etc. Expand the bar graph experience by graphing birthday months, favorite subjects, eye color, and any personal subject that appeals to students. Later on, pie and bar graphs can be utilized to visually demonstrate concepts in social studies, science, etc. For instance, create a bar graph to show average temperatures for each month so students can see the flow of the seasons.

Time lines are another graphic organizer helpful to student learning. They can begin with their own histories with the *Family Time Line* on page 60 and from there, expand to an *Autobiographic Time Line* on pages 61 and 62, the latter being useful for learning more about the lives of historical figures, as well as fictional characters. A *Pyramid* is useful, once more (beginning on page 63, in this section), as a means of organizing information on a main idea (*Main Idea Pyramid*, page 64). Locate examples of other pyramids for students to examine, such as food pyramids. *Book Report Pyramids* (pages 65 and 66) and the *Story Pyramid* (page 67) are simple and versatile for students learning how to distinguish what information is pertinent. The three versions included are adaptable to your students' abilities.

The section returns to another kind of pie, the *Why? Pie* on pages 68 and 69. The Why? Pie, encourages students to listen and pay attention, and encourages their natural curiosities. You may wish to introduce the Why? Pie concept with a brainstorming session and a demonstration. The best learning takes place when students are curious and motivated to find the answers to their questions.

The *Senses Matrix* (pages 70 and 71), is useful in expanding student awareness and use of their senses in writing. It is also useful in helping them to see, at a glance, how important are our senses. While the most logical use of this matrix may be in creative writing or science, try it for history, to add a sense of immediacy and a sense of place to studies. Try it for geography, meteorology, and journal writing.

How I Spend My Day

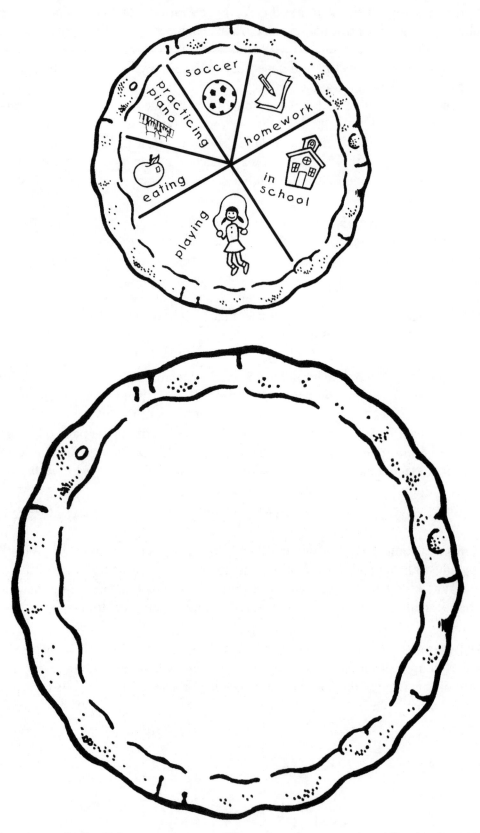

58

Our Favorite Colors

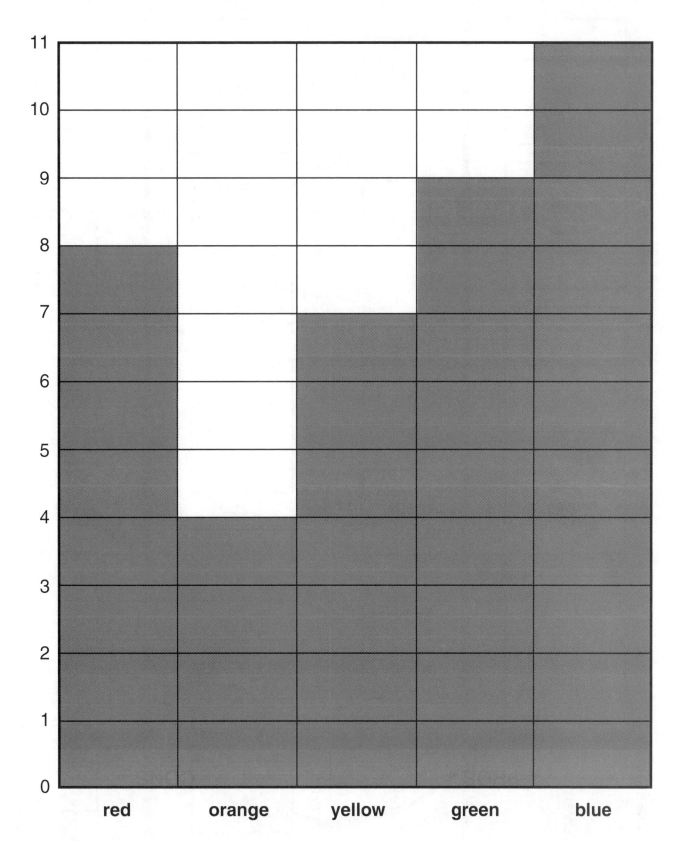

Family Time Line

Example

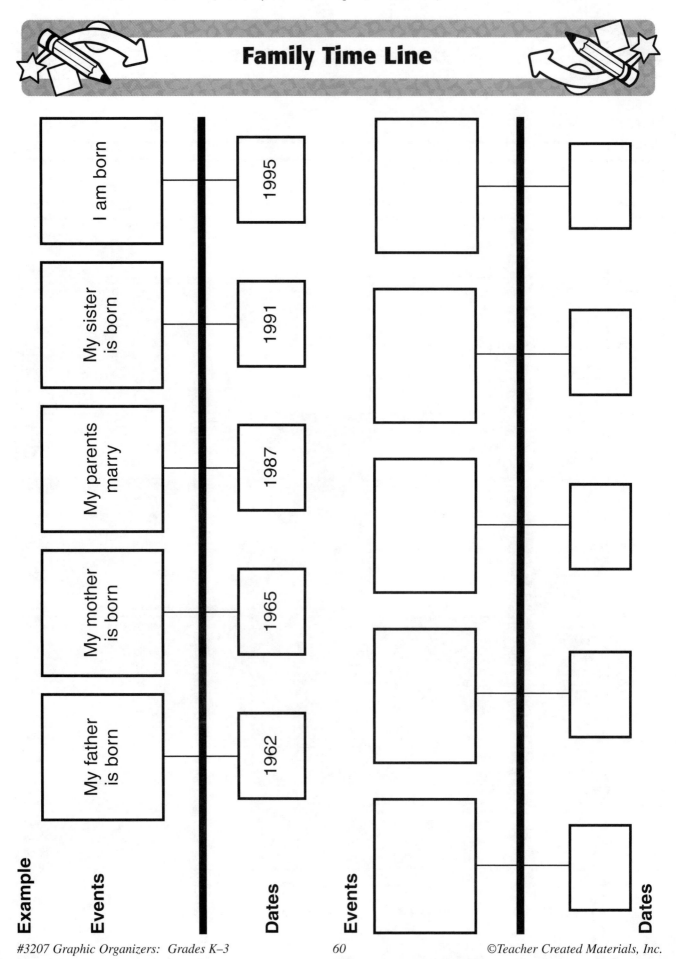

Events

| I am born | My sister is born | My parents marry | My mother is born | My father is born |

Dates

| 1995 | 1991 | 1987 | 1965 | 1962 |

Events

Dates

Autobiographic Time Line

Here is an example of an autobiographic time line created by a student about herself.

August 4, 1994	I was born.
January 20, 1995	My first tooth.
February 1995	I could sit up and crawl.
July 1995	I took my first steps.
June 1997	I had my first ballet class.
September 1999	I went to kindergarten.
May 2000	I had my first ballet recital.
February 2001	I got my kitten "Phoofie."
December 2002	Our family moved to another state.
February 2003	I found a new ballet school.
August 2003	I made a new friend, and she came to my birthday party.

You can also use a time line like this to organize information about a person from history, or a fictional character from a book.

Autobiographic Time Line

Date Event

Pyramid

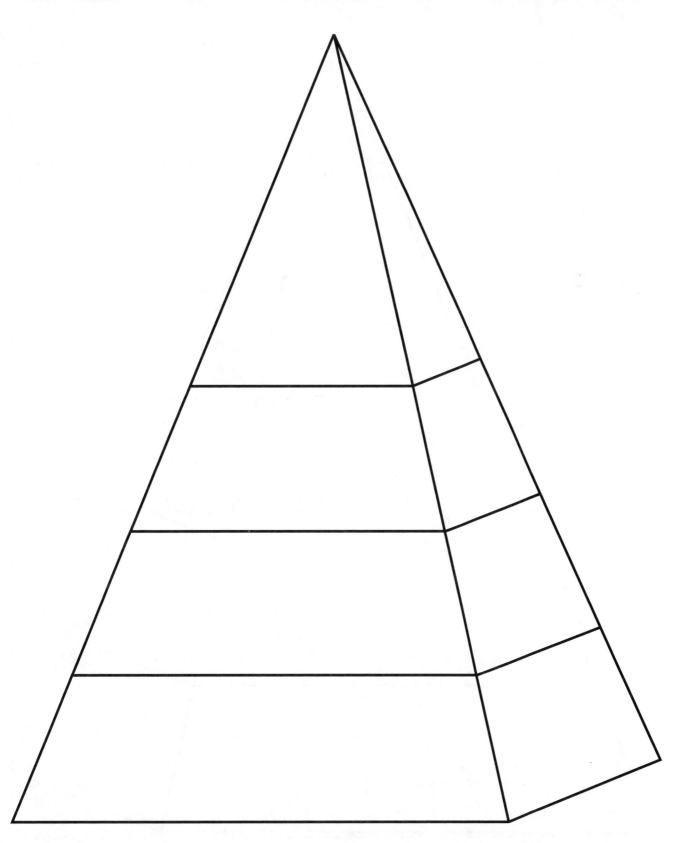

Main Idea Pyramid

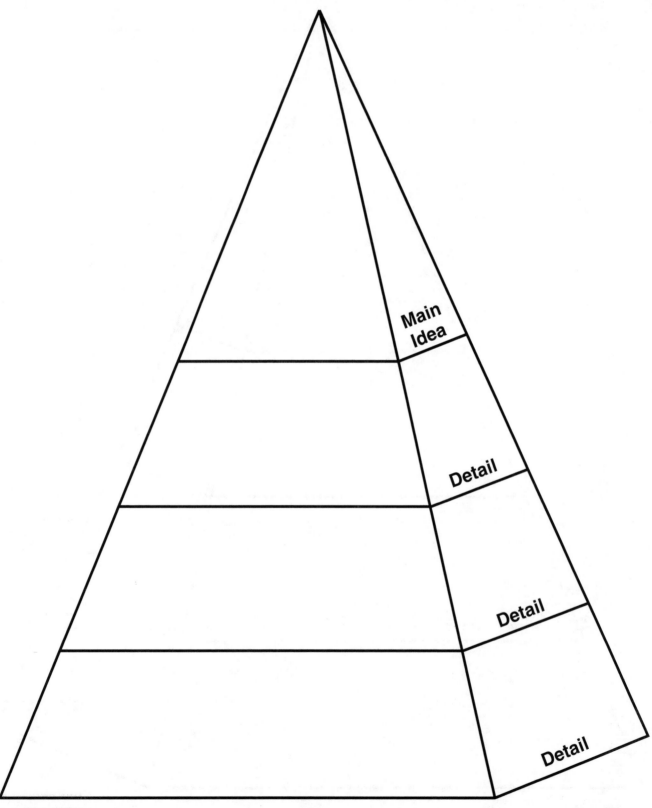

Book Report Pyramid I

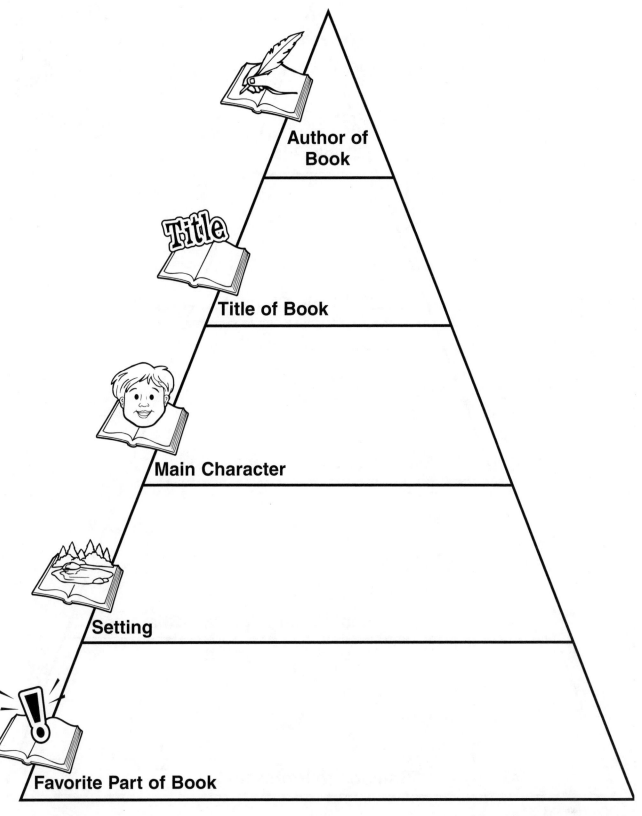

Author of
Book

Title of Book

Main Character

Setting

Favorite Part of Book

Book Report Pyramid II

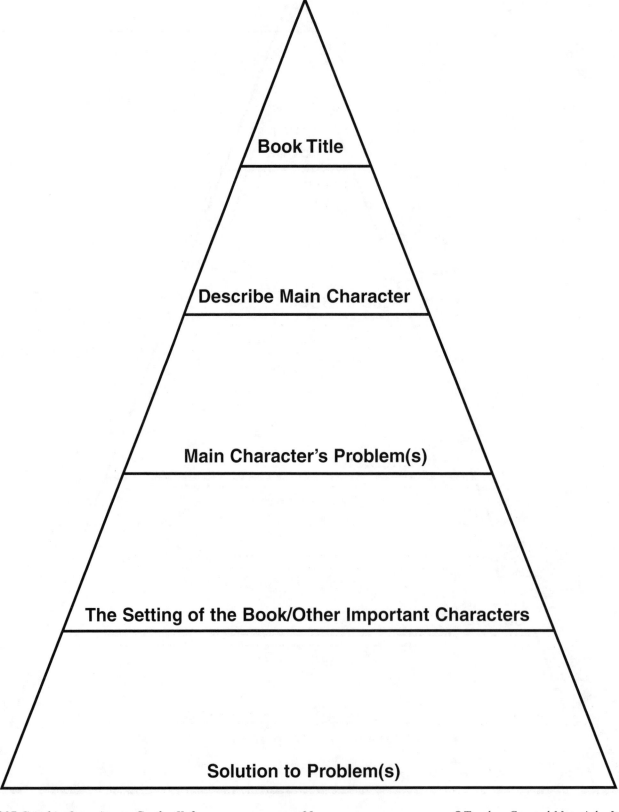

Book Title

Describe Main Character

Main Character's Problem(s)

The Setting of the Book/Other Important Characters

Solution to Problem(s)

Story Pyramid

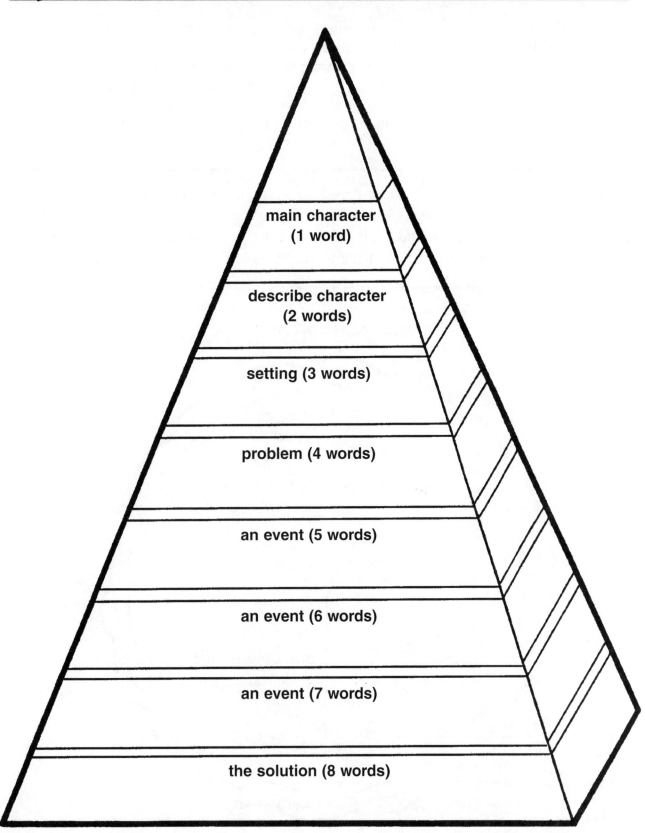

main character
(1 word)

describe character
(2 words)

setting (3 words)

problem (4 words)

an event (5 words)

an event (6 words)

an event (7 words)

the solution (8 words)

Why? Pie

You can use the Why? Pie strategy to help students identify essential relationships between objects or concepts. Using the worksheet on page 69, model the strategy by having students read an expository passage and then ask questions that begin with the word *Why* and can only be answered by inference (the answer is not directly stated in the article). Then have students read further and work in pairs to come up with *why* questions about the material and to discuss possible responses to their questions. After that they can exchange questions with another pair and develop responses to those questions as well. Here's an example of a student's Why? Pie after reading this article:

> Floods happen when too much water runs into a stream or river. The stream or river gets so high it goes right over its banks. Floods drown people and animals. Floods can wash away houses, cars, and bridges. They hurt crops and carry away topsoil. For thousands of years people have tried to stop floods.

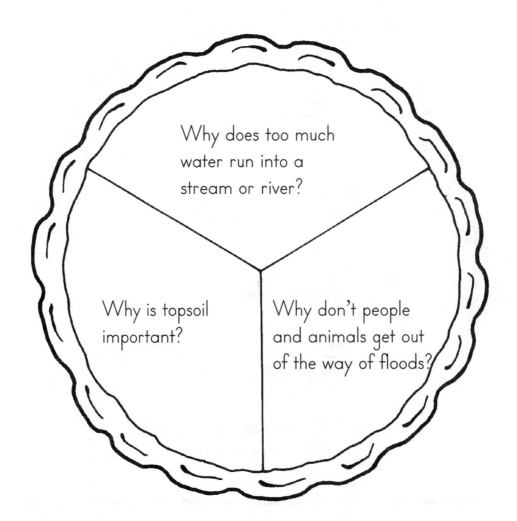

Why? Pie

 **Senses Matrix**

Senses Matrix

What It Is	Looks Like	Smells Like	Feels Like	Tastes Like	Sounds Like
Thanksgiving	red, gold, and brown leaves	turkey and pumpkin pie in the oven	warm and cozy sweaters and hugs	tangy cranberry sauce smooth mashed potatoes	people talking and laughing glasses clinking and plates scraping
School	black asphalt and green grass brick building	glue and pens cafeteria cooking lunch	rough hand ball hard desks	cafeteria pizzas salt and flour dough	loud bells ringing noisy kids talking
Summer	blue green yellow	the ocean rubber flip flops sweat sunscreen	warm and lazy floating on water	hotdogs watermelon	birds singing ocean roaring giggling
My Baby Brother	fat and round drooly smiles	baby powder baby musk	soft and wet	salty like strained peas	giggles loud wails

Senses Matrix

Senses Matrix

Sounds Like				
Tastes Like				
Feels Like				
Smells Like				
Looks Like				
What It Is				

And the Point Is . . .

It is very important for students to comprehend, as soon as they are able to, the concept of a thesis or main idea, and supporting points. It is a template, as it were, that they will use throughout their school careers. Their ability to visualize this concept early on will enable them to be strong students when it is time to express their ideas in a variety of forums, especially the thesis essay. To ease young students into this concept, the section begins with an opportunity for each student to draw his or her main point (*A Picture About My Topic*, page 73). For beginners, skip the organizer and, after a discussion of topics, have them simply draw a picture of the topic. Then, have them dictate what they wish to say about the topic. Instruct them that what they are doing is demonstrating the main topic and the supporting details.

Main Street (pages 74 and 75) is a picture organizer that will help students to visualize the concept of a main idea and the details. Encourage students to take the main street concept a bit further by drawing a map with a main highway and side streets. They can label the routes and illustrate them.

The target on page 76 (*On Target)* will help students visualize the importance of the main idea bull's eye. A game of magnetic darts can reinforce this concept. Have each student write his or her main idea in the center circle with the details becoming more plentiful the further out within the concentric circles. Page 77, *Tree Trunk Organizer*, is another way for students to visualize and organize their ideas.

With the *Jellyfish Organizer*, on page 78, students are introduced to more complex graphs and mind maps. Show the students pictures of jellyfish to reinforce the concept. They may wish to create an organizer that looks more like a jellyfish, but be sure to keep the basic structure the same. The Jellyfish Organizer is useful for older students as well, as it is a template for a typical five-paragraph essay.

Webs are always useful for visually graphing the main idea and its offshoots. *A Web to Point the Way* is included for this purpose on page 79. The organizer, *What Happened?* (page 80), is a good way for young students to gain familiarity with the tried and true Ws and H that they will return to throughout their schooling. Use this graph for current events, history, classroom newsletters, as well as book characters and book reports. The *T-Bar* (page 81) is a quick draw graph that students can use even when they do not have a printed graphic organizer to use, and as such, should be useful to them for years to come.

Good things come in boxes of all sizes and students will find *Boxes of Ideas* (page 82) to be a memorable, visual way to organize ideas. To reinforce the concept of many details supporting one large idea, use actual boxes as a visual aid. When the boxes are labeled with one large box resting securely upon several, well-placed smaller boxes, they will get the idea.

Discuss opinions with students. Present them with a topic about which they would have strong feelings, such as doing away with recess (yes or no?) or video games. Have students choose a stance and write, or dictate their opinions, reasons for their opinions, and conclusions on the *This Is What I Think* organizer found on page 83. Post many different opinions on a bulletin board display. The controversial topics may be good ones to use in learning to write supporting details for an opinion essay. The *Paragraph Organizer* on page 84 will be helpful for beginning writers with strong opinions who are ready to write about them.

A Picture About My Topic

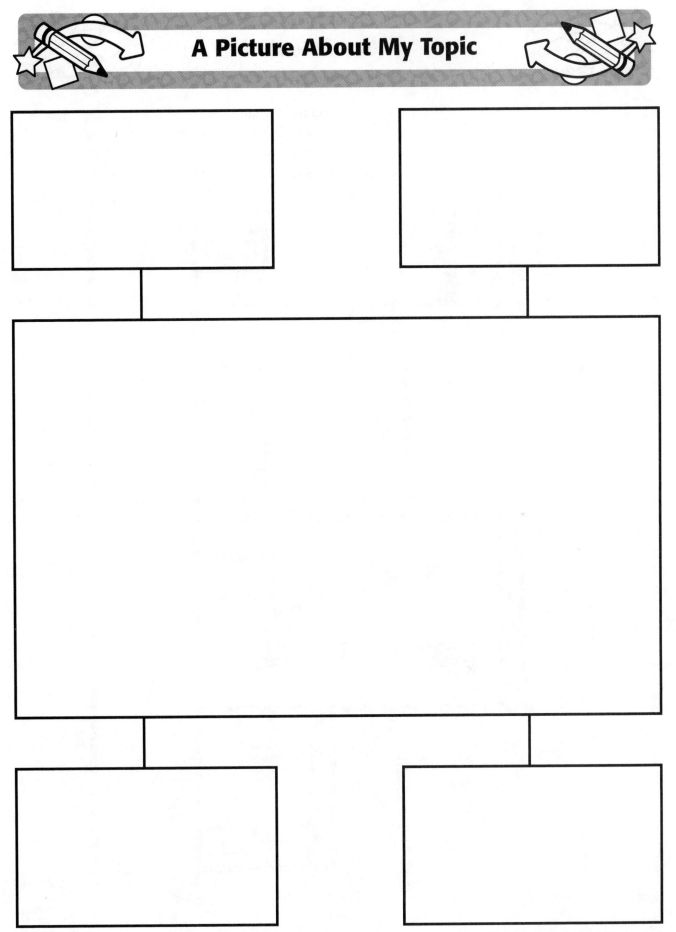

Main Street

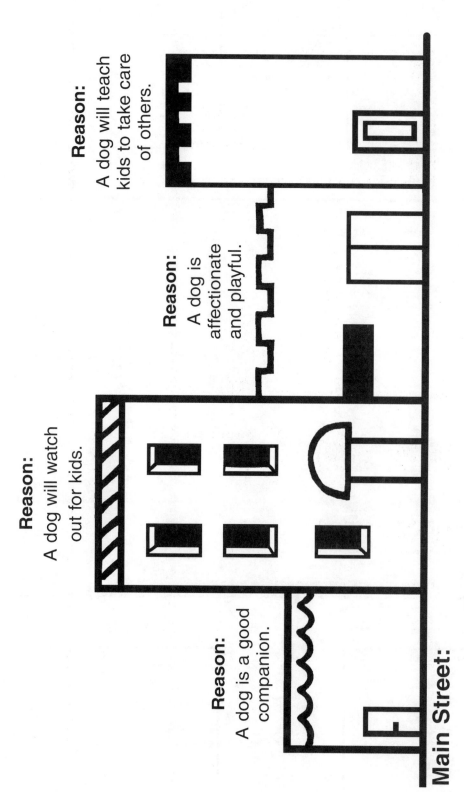

Reason: A dog will teach kids to take care of others.

Reason: A dog is affectionate and playful.

Reason: A dog will watch out for kids.

Reason: A dog is a good companion.

Main Street: There are many reasons why a dog is a good pet for kids.

Main Street

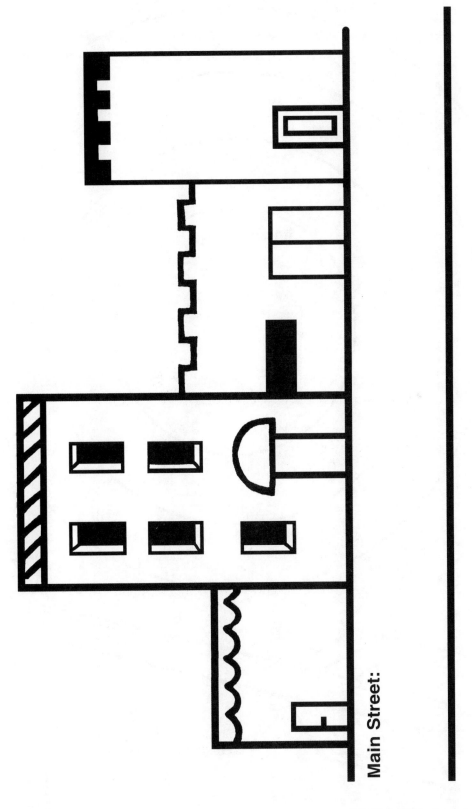

Main Street:

On Target

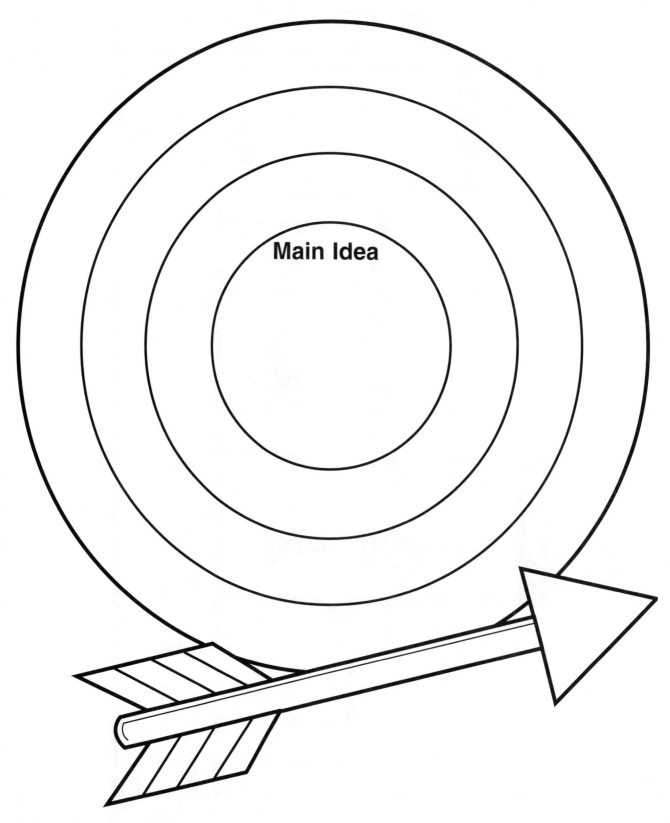

Main Idea

Tree Trunk Organizer

TOPIC

Jellyfish Organizer

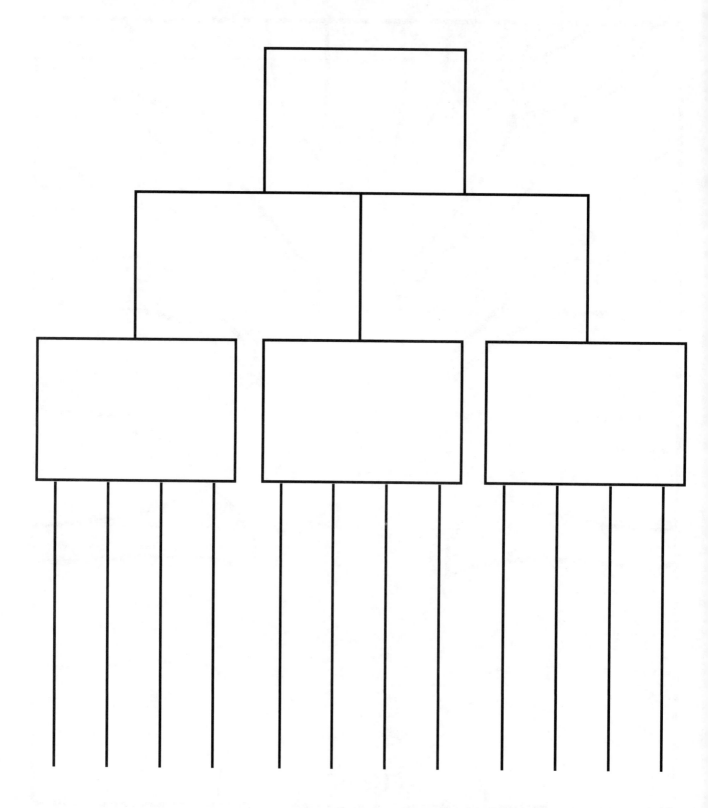

A Web to Point the Way

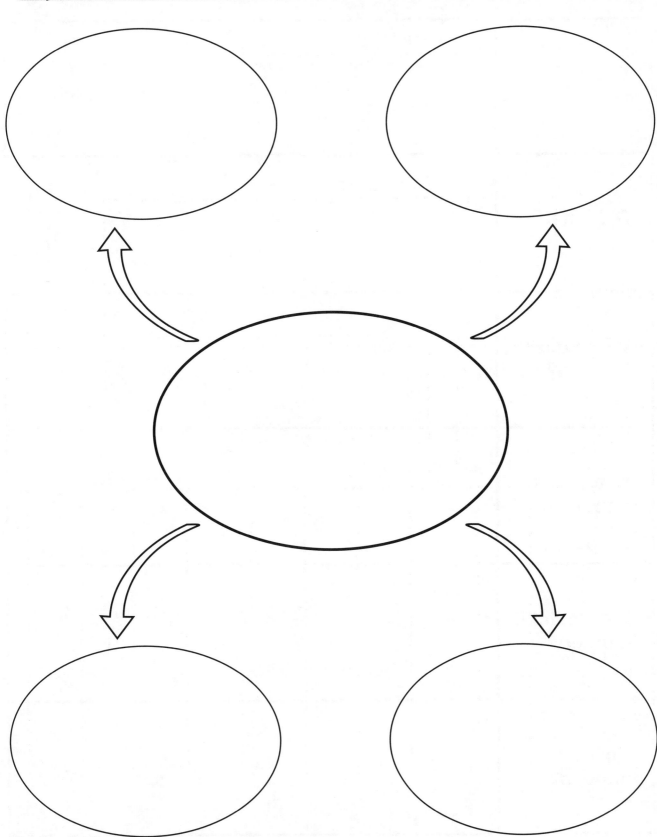

What Happened?

What or who?	
Did what?	
When did it happen?	
Why did it happen?	
Where did it happen?	
How did it happen?	

T-Bar

My main idea is:

These are the details:

Boxes of Ideas

The Main Idea

Detail

Detail

Detail

This Is What I Think

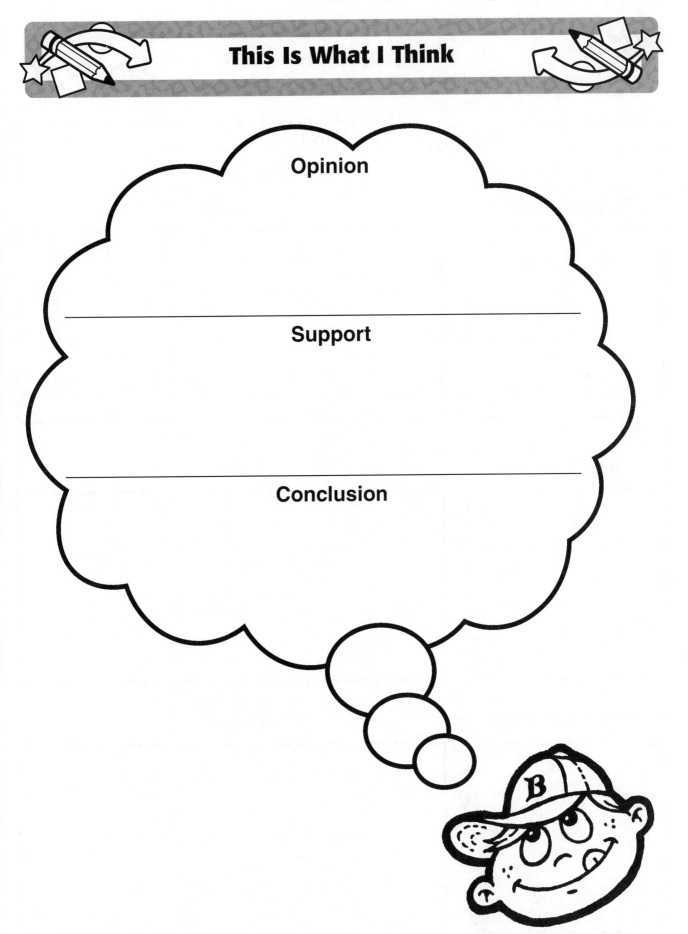

Opinion

Support

Conclusion

Paragraph Organizer

The Main Topic

_____

Supporting Topic

Details

Supporting Topic

Details

Supporting Topic

Details

Having a Plan in Mind

Students are introduced to the concept of mind mapping with the simple *5 Ws and 1 H Web* (page 86) with which this section begins. With practice, and this web, students will gain competency in organizing and visualizing information, thoughts, and ideas. Such webs make the transition between an idea that comes to mind and getting the idea on paper.

Preview and Predict (page 87) is a deceptively simple graphic organizer that enables students to wonder about and be curious about future learning. It teaches them to look for clues, which will facilitate future researching skills. It is also an introduction to the Know/Want to Know/Wonder or Learned concept that is so effective in learning new things and in encouraging curiosity. And, furthermore, it is also another opportunity for young students to express their thoughts by drawing. It is only a logical extension to include a *K-W-L Plan* (page 88) at this point. Use it for a variety of activities and subjects. You may even want to have students use such a form daily, before and after seeing a film on a subject, before and after an interview of a community worker, an oral book report, or research.

What a Character! (page 89) is meant to be used as a form of book reporting or thinking about fictional characters, however, it may also be used for historical biographies, interviews of fellow students or family members. Students may inadvertently learn some new words while having fun using the organizer, *I Know What That Means!* (page 90). You may wish to have these forms in notebooks for each student, or as individual forms that students may use at will. As incentive, filled-in forms might be placed in a special deposit box for a weekly prize drawing of pencils, cute erasers, etc. Students will learn to use contextual clues to find meanings of words. Encourage them to add additional definitions even when they guessed correctly.

5 Ws and 1 H Web

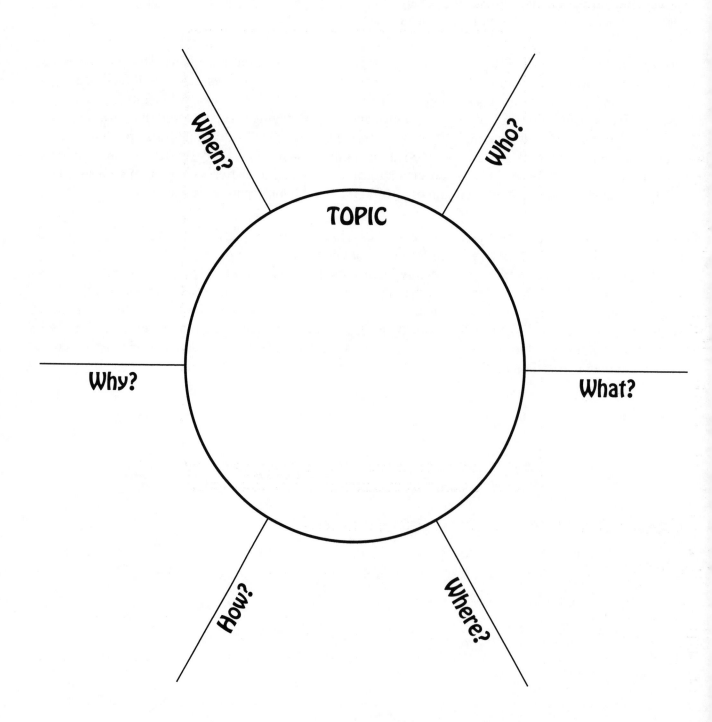

TOPIC

When?

Who?

Why?

What?

How?

Where?

Preview and Predict

Directions: Write the title of the book you are going to read below.

Draw the cover of the book.

Predict: What do you think you will learn?

I predict: _____

_____

_____

_____

_____

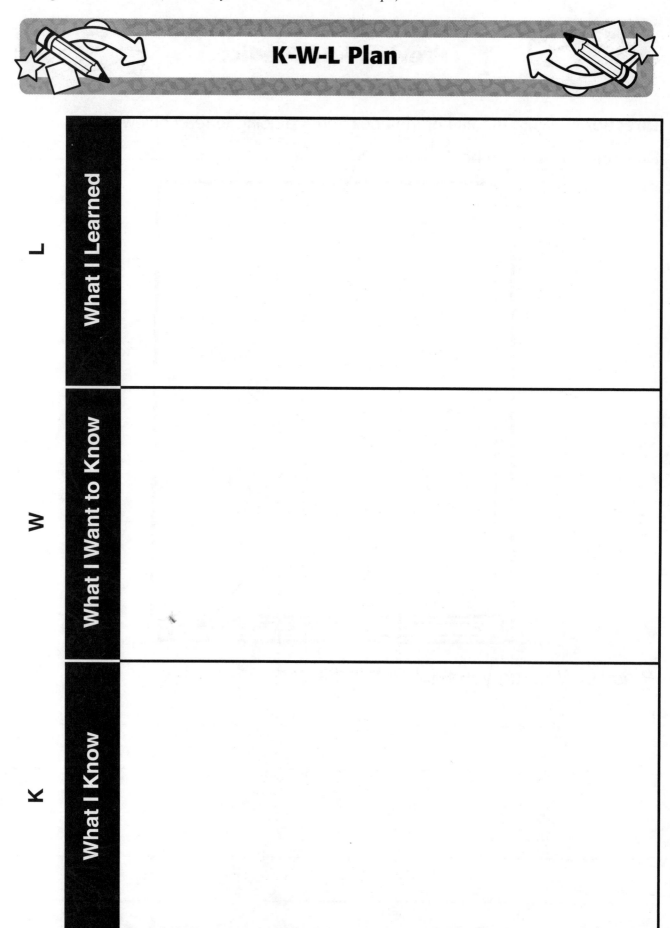

K-W-L Plan

L — What I Learned

W — What I Want to Know

K — What I Know

What a Character!

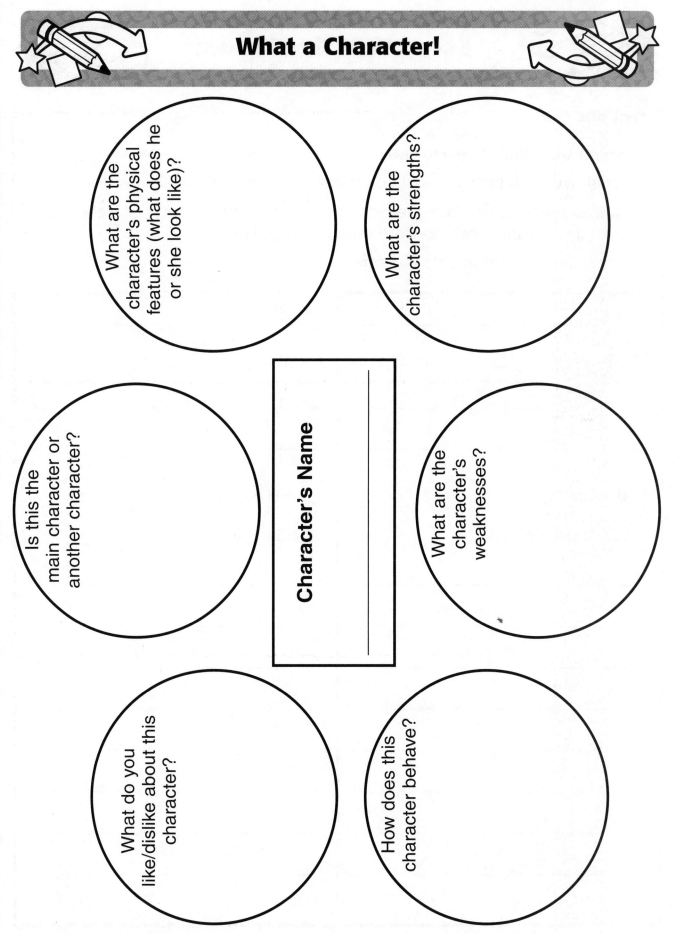

What are the character's physical features (what does he or she look like)?

What are the character's strengths?

Is this the main character or another character?

Character's Name

What are the character's weaknesses?

What do you like/dislike about this character?

How does this character behave?

I Know What That Means!

Directions

1. Find a word that is new to you.

2. Write what you think it means on the "My guess" line.

3. Now look up the words in the dictionary. If your guess was right, check the box. If not, write what the word means on the line.

4. Find another word and do the same.

Word: _____	Word: _____
My guess: _____	My guess: _____
_____	_____
_____	_____
I guessed right! ❏	I guessed right! ❏
Now I know it means _____	Now I know it means _____
_____	_____
_____	_____
_____	_____
_____	_____
_____	_____
_____	_____

Organized Fun

A student's favorite subject is, of course, him or herself! *Look at Me!* (page 92) may be the best graphic organizer to begin with, as it will be easy for students to fill in the information to create the shape-body. Have younger students dictate their responses and have students of all ages draw a self-portrait in the circle at the top. These organizers would make a great display around the room, especially at the beginning of the school year. *My Own Coat of Arms* (page 93) is similar in that it is fun for students to create a work of art about their own lives. The same organizer may be extended when applied to historical or fictional subjects.

On page 94, there is a *Picture Glossary* that will encourage reading of all kinds, organizing, vocabulary development, while having fun drawing. Create year-long notebooks so that students will have picture glossaries to keep and peruse. Lifelong habits of organizational skills will be the end result. The *Acrostic Grid*, found on page 95, will be useful for many subjects. To use, choose a topic, or have students choose a topic, and write it down the left-hand column. For instance, T-R-E-E-S. All lines need not be used, and the grid can be expanded for more capable students. For each line, students will add words, phrases, sentences, or even the lines of a poem to utilize that letter of the alphabet. For instance, T = tall, R = red, E = elegant, E = evergreen, S = shade.

Page 96 features a blank *Comic Strip*. It may be used for vocabulary word use, to illustrate an event in a student's life, or an event in history. It may also be used for sequencing: steps in a how-to, or the order of the school day, etc. with characters describing what is happening. For fun, let students try creating a funny cartoon strip.

Look at Me!

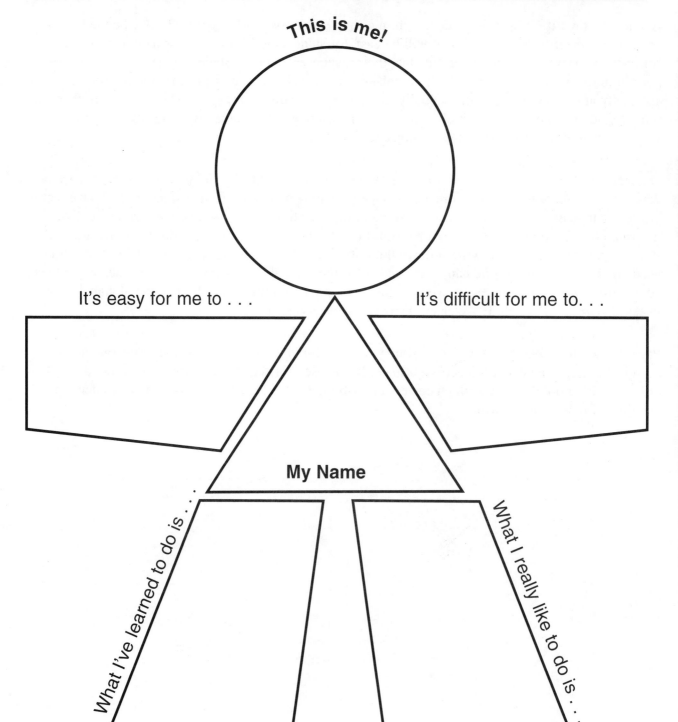

This is me!

It's easy for me to . . .

It's difficult for me to. . .

My Name

What I've learned to do is . . .

What I really like to do is . . .

What I want to do

in the future is . . .

My Own Coat of Arms

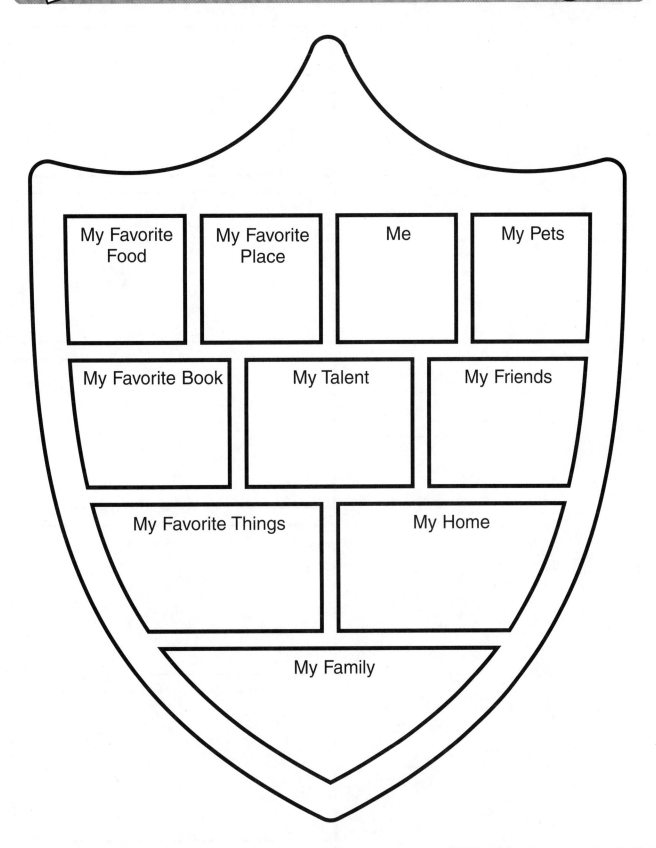

My Favorite Food

My Favorite Place

Me

My Pets

My Favorite Book

My Talent

My Friends

My Favorite Things

My Home

My Family

Picture Glossary

1. _____

2. _____

3. _____

4. _____

5. _____

Acrostic Grid

Comic Strip